THE CURIOUS **KIDS'** *ACTIVITY B*

BOREDOM BUSTERS!

AVERY HART & PAUL MANTELL

■

Illustrated by Loretta Trezzo Braren

WILLIAMSON PUBLISHING • CHARLOTTE, VT 05445

Kids Can!®, *Little Hands®*, and *Tales Alive!®* are
registered trademarks of Williamson Publishing
Company.
Kaleidoscope Kids™ is a trademark of Williamson
Publishing Company.

Library of Congress
Cataloging-in-Publication Data
Hart, Avery.
   Boredom busters! : the curious kids' activity book /
Avery Hart and Paul Mantell.
       p.   cm.
   "A Williamson kids can! book"—Cover.
   Includes index.
   Summary: Suggests a variety of both indoor and
outdoor activities which relate to nature, the
environment, ecology, music, sky watching, backyard
fun, the neighborhood, and the wider world.
   ISBN 1-885593-15-5
   1. Creative activities and seat work—United
States—Juvenile literature. 2. Amusements—United
States—Juvenile literature. 3. Nature study—United
States—Juvenile literature.
   [1. Handicraft. 2. Amusements. 3. Nature study.]
I. Mantell, Paul.   II. Title.
GV1204.12.H36   1997
790.1'922—dc21   97-19370
                                      CIP
                                      AC

Cover design: Trezzo-Braren Studio
Illustrations: Loretta Trezzo
Page design: Trezzo-Braren Studio
Printing: Capital City Press

Williamson Publishing Co.
P.O. Box 185
Charlotte, Vermont 05445
800–234–8791

Manufactured in the United States of America

10 9 8 7 6 5 4 3 2

CONTENTS

Dedication

For our children and our parents —
wonderful people to spend weekends with.

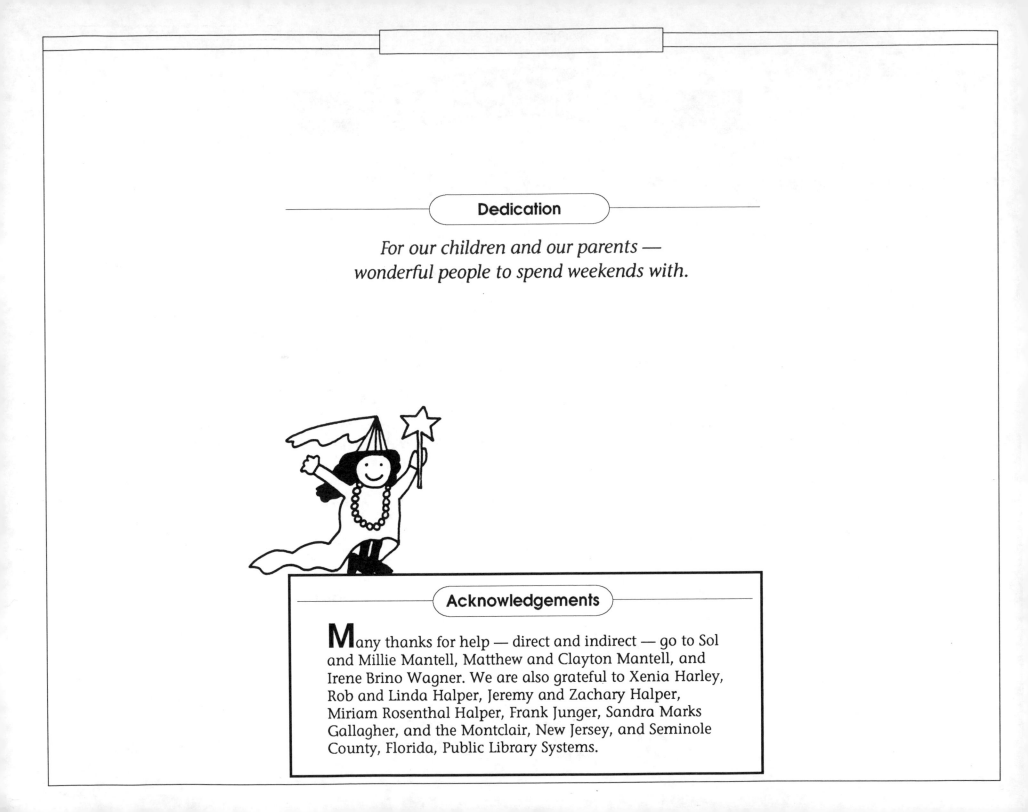

Acknowledgements

Many thanks for help — direct and indirect — go to Sol and Millie Mantell, Matthew and Clayton Mantell, and Irene Brino Wagner. We are also grateful to Xenia Harley, Rob and Linda Halper, Jeremy and Zachary Halper, Miriam Rosenthal Halper, Frank Junger, Sandra Marks Gallagher, and the Montclair, New Jersey, and Seminole County, Florida, Public Library Systems.

FOREWORD

Ahhh, it's Friday afternoon, everybody's favorite day of the week. Why? Because we'll soon be off work, school will be out, and we'll finally have a chance to "do our own thing" for a couple of days.

Now, maybe you're the type who doesn't need any help with your weekends. You already know how you are going to spend your time — laying on the couch, munching junk food, watching TV, and playing video games . . . .

Or maybe you're the type whose schedule is crammed to the gills in advance, with meetings of this club and that team, and visits to relatives and friends . . . .

But maybe, just maybe, you're looking for something new to try. Maybe you're sick of TV, and the same old weekend snore. Maybe you're the type who likes to explore new things to do — or maybe you'd like to become that type! In fact, maybe you'd like your whole family to become that type!

Well, if you are, then this book is for you. It's for anybody who wants to make his or her weekends into refreshing, renewing, wild and wonderful days of discovery.

Weekends are the absolute best time for discovering — yourself, your family, your community and that wide world out there, too.

So, read on, explorers! If you thought weekends were just the pause between Friday and Monday, think again . . . !

HOW TO USE THIS BOOK

You'll notice from the Table of Contents that there are several different sections in this book, each with a number of activities listed underneath. Some of these activities could have gone into other sections instead — for instance, a Bug Hunt is just as much a part of Back To Nature as it is a part of Backyard Fun. So you'll just have to give the book a good "leafing through" before settling on any activities to try.

The activities in this book were all selected with certain things in mind:

Safety and fun. We tried out a lot of activities for this book, and if they weren't fun and safe, they didn't get in! We hope you'll agree with us about ones which passed the test. Many are child-tested, by our boys and their friends, who are expert "fun explorers."

Price. Everything in this book is either free or extremely inexpensive. Having a good time over the weekend doesn't have to cost a fortune.

Simplicity. Nothing in this book is so complicated that it will be frustrating, and it's all been tested for clean-up ease. Weekends are for fun — not drudgery!

Harmony and help for the environment. Let's face it, nature can use some extra care these days. Who better to give it than kids and their families? Exploring and working with nature is not only satisfying, but vital.

Equip your household for fun

You won't need much in the way of special equipment to do the things in this book. The supplies are as simple and everyday as we could find — things like scissors, glue, and paint. Hobby shops sell inexpensive, ready-made paint kits that are handy to use and store. White wall paint can become any color you want just by adding a little food coloring. Keep your art supplies together on a shelf, or in a drawer or cabinet.

When you set up a project, always have a damp, clean rag close by. On the spot cleanups, even of glue and paint, are a snap.

It also helps if you hang onto any cartons, boxes, jars, and jugs that find their way into your life. Use cartons to store "reusables" — or maybe we should call them "creatables." Things like toilet paper cardboards, cleaned-out milk cartons, and shoeboxes, come in handy in lots of ways when you're exploring and doing things with kids. (Our garbage load got much reduced as we created the projects!)

Large sides of cartons make super-light, portable workspaces, too.

Cross-references

Occasionally you'll see something like this: (see Classy Gifts To Make, page 156). That means you can find more on the subject if you turn to the page listed. However, if you're really interested in something in a big way, we recommend a trip to the library.

Finally . . .

Don't be afraid to experiment or try your own twists on some of the activities we've included. And don't forget to ask a friend to come along on your adventures, either.

You'll find there really is a pot of gold at the end of the weekend — it's you — by yourself, or with people you like, doing, discovering, exploring, and having fun!

AVERY AND PAUL

ENVIRONMENTALLY YOURS

Make a Home Recycling Center

Do you want to stop pollution and save money, too? Then start *recycling*! Everybody's doing it — all over the country and throughout the world!

Recycling means collecting items so they can be used again and again. It's the important new game in town, and it's growing all the time, as people discover more and more things that can be re-used.

And here's more good news. Recycling is positively habit-forming! Once you get a good system in gear, collecting items for re-use just gets easier and easier.

GETTING CONNECTED

You're probably already connected to a recycling program of some sort. Your town sanitation department may have a program to collect metal, plastic, and paper right at your curb. If it doesn't, donate some time from your weekend to a kid-published newspaper. (See page 113.) When enough people ask for curbside recycling, it will happen.

But even if your town is not yet actively involved in recycling, you can be! Check the yellow pages of your phone book, or call your local town offices. They'll know of a volunteer group or business that is working on recycling in your area.

Everything in its place — including the recyclables!

To get your home recycling center started, you'll need to establish a recycling center in your house or apartment, and you'll need three or four large cartons or baskets. The kitchen is a good place to collect plastic, metal, and glass. If you have a pantry, the floor is excellent for a recycling center. Or look for some free space close to the trash, or under a sink. Try to make the place you use for collecting as convenient as possible. Mark each box for glass, metal, paper, and plastics. Then, whenever you're finished with a recyclable, rinse it off and toss it in the appropriate carton. It's that simple.

Can and bottle deposits

If your state has a deposit law, you can get money for rinsed out glass and metal containers! Just bring them back to the place you bought them, or any other place that sells the same item, and you will be given money for each can or bottle! (You can get together with your friends and neighbors to raise extra money, too. See Neighborhood Recycling, page 16.)

Drop-off center

Until you get curbside recycling, you may have to drop off your recyclables at a neighborhood center. This won't be so difficult if you store your recyclables in the trunk of the car as they start to pile up indoors. Or, store the overflow in your garage or basement.

Look up the center on a local map. Does anyone in the family have errands to run near it? If so, drop off your recyclables along your route. If the center is a little out of the way, just go once a month. That's a good time to reward the whole family for being such high-minded global citizens, too. Why not combine your recycling drop-offs with a trip to a pizza parlor?

Organize a recycling game for little kids

Older children can help younger ones learn about recycling by playing this game. You'll need a pillowcase, four cartons, and a bunch of household stuff.

Mark the cartons RE-USE, RECYCLE, COMPOST, and GIVE AWAY, and line them up in a row. If the child can't read, draw an appropriate picture on the box, too.

Then give the younger child a pillowcase full of "garbage." Be sure to include a beverage can, a plastic bottle, a shirt or pair of child's shoes in good condition, part of a newspaper, and something to represent kitchen scraps, like a plastic banana or orange. Put at least six items into the pillowcase.

Tell the child what you know about recycling and why it's important, and show her each carton and what it's for.

Now it's time for the child to play. Tell her to place the things in her pillowcase into the right cartons. If she goes to the wrong carton, gently correct her and help her find the right one. (Many items can be re-used or recycled, depending on your area.) When she's all finished, applaud her and give her a reward, like a hug, or a sticker.

The more you can teach younger children the right way to sort out their "garbage," the less actual garbage there will be!

Giving it away

Before you know it, it'll be second nature to think "second-hand." And the more you spread the word about recycling, re-using, and making the most of everything we use, the better this world will be to live in!

Even this book was written by recycled people. We were once kids and now we've been recycled into grown-ups!

DISCOVER THE THRILL OF SUPERMARKET SLEUTHING

Will the floor polish reveal its deadly secret? Are the frozen dinners horribly overpriced? Just how many chemicals are in that cupcake? Does that can of "juice" actually contain juice? As a supermarket spy, you are about to find out!

You are about to enter the world of the weekend shopping spy . . . . It's a trip to the supermarket filled with suspense and drama. You will uncover information and decode it. This information will not only save money — it may very well improve someone's health!

For the mission, should you choose to accept it, you and your fellow operatives will be issued a powerful weapon. It's called money. The weapon is activated by choosing when — and when not — to spend it. Remember: the way you use this weapon gives you power even over giant corporations. Corporations need you to buy their products! Their very survival is up to you!

THE TASK: UNCOVER, SEARCH, AND DESTROY

Hidden in the supermarket are super-spy messages. Before you can understand them, you've got to find them. These secret messages have been cleverly hidden. They are written in tiny print on the sides and bottoms of packages. They are hidden amidst large print promises and bold claims. They are disguised in a way designed to throw consumers off the trail of the truth and lure them into a money trap. Don't let it happen to you!

TARGET TERMS TO BE WARY OF:

NATURAL, ALL NATURAL
You will see this word everywhere in the supermarket. Too often it's put on products in a prominent way to attract buyers. The trouble is, it doesn't mean anything!

FREE BONUS OR PRIZE
Most free prizes or bonuses wind up costing you money in the end, one way or another. See if you can spot the trick!

SUGAR-FREE
A lot of products that claim to be sugar-free actually have large amounts of artificial sweeteners. Or they use honey, maplesyrup, or corn syrup — highly concentrated forms of simple sugars. Just one more reason to do some careful sleuthing.

ENRICHED
This word is often used on bread products. Unfortunately, it doesn't mean a thing. Enriched flour just means that *some, but not all* of the nutrients that were taken out in processing have been put back in. Look for whole grains instead.

LITE OR LOW-FAT
Advertisers use these phrases because high fat diets were implicated in all kinds of deadly diseases. To calculate the amount of calories that come from fat in a product, multiply the fat gram number by 9. Then divide that number into the total calories. The results of your mathematical sleuthing may reveal a manufacturer's deceit!

OTHER ADVERTISING TERMS TO BE WARY OF:
Fresh
Premium
New (or All-New)
Improved
Cholesterol-free

Come as you aren't

A British accent, a Russian accent, a Southern drawl, a moustache, a trench coat to conceal your secret weapon — a pen — to take down information, a magnifying glass, and even a licorice pipe, should you be lucky enough to have one — all these enhance a supermarket spying trip. If you are making the trip with your fellow operatives, split up into teams. Perhaps your mother can pretend she is an ordinary shopper, while you search and destroy the most toxic substances by *not buying* them.

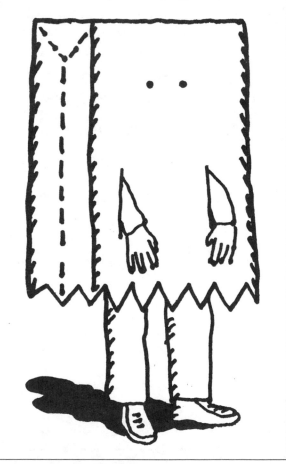

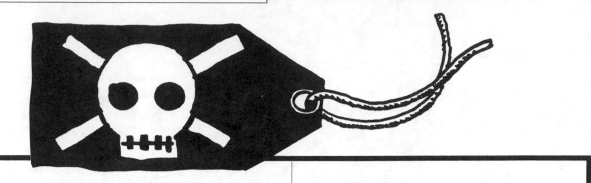

Danger — poison for sale!

Here's a list of potentially dangerous or toxic substances found in food and common household products. Avoid them like the plague! Artificial colors and flavors are made in laboratories and serve absolutely no purpose in food. Some of them may be harmless; some cause problems if you use a lot of them. And no one is absolutely sure that they're safe to consume over a lifetime. Stay away from them for safety's sake. Everything else on the list has been proven to be dangerous.

Artificial colors and flavors (especially Blue #1 & 2, Red #2, 3, and 40, Green #3, Yellow #5 & 6.

Sodium nitrite

Sodium nitrate

Saccharin

Monosodium glutamate (MSG)

Di-ethylene glycol

Nitrobenzene

Ammonia

Phosphates

Sodium hydroxide (and Potassium hydroxide)

Sulfites

The friendly preservatives

Here's some good news! Not all substances added to products are bad for you. Here are some additive good guys that actually enhance your health!

Ascorbic acid, sodium ascorbate

Beta-carotene

Citric acid, sodium citrate

Riboflavin, riboflavin phosphate

Pantothenic acid, calcium pantothenate

Hydrolyzed vegetable protein (HVP)

Folacin

PRECYCLING: BEWARE OF OVERPACKAGING!

Products that come in fancy, individually-wrapped containers aren't always the best value for you or for Planet Earth. Those fancy packages are often designed to be tossed away after the product is opened. That adds to the world's garbage unnecessarily.

Remember, you're paying for the package, too, as well as the product. Is it really something you want to spend money on? Probably not.

Join the world of *precycling*. Avoid buying disposable products. Instead, look for products that come in recyclable, reuseable, or refillable containers.

A FINAL WORD:
PAPER OR PLASTIC?

Okay, so you're done shopping. But there's still one last part of your mission. On the checkout line, the cashier will ask you whether you want your purchases packed in paper or plastic bags. Which do you choose? What's the smart decision?

There's trouble with both choices, actually. Paper produces PCBs and other serious pollutants when it's made. Plastic is a problem on the other end, when you throw it away. Most plastic is non-biodegradable, and clogs landfills. So what do you do?

First, ask the cashier if the supermarket takes back used plastic bags for recycling. If it does, choose plastic. If not, choose whichever you can make the most use of at home.

The best solution, however, is to bring your own bags! Canvas, cloth, or mesh bags are inexpensive, and can be washed and reused again and again!

BUYER BEWARE!!! Watch out for these words— SUCROSE, GLUCOSE, DEXTROSE, FRUCTOSE, MALTOSE, LACTOSE. They are just other ways of saying SUGAR.

PLANT A TREE

OAK · MAPLE · CHESTNUT · PINE

Good friends

Trees and people go together. Trees breathe out oxygen that we breathe in! They need carbon dioxide that we breathe out! In the most basic and true way, trees keep the air healthy for people. Yet, sad to say, over the past hundred years, as the human population has exploded, more and more trees have been cut down all over the globe.

Well, the time has come to right that wrong! It's important for people to plant more and more trees. Trees add oxygen to the air. They take carbon dioxide out of the air. They shade us in hot weather, and provide places for birds to nest, and for people to meet. And that's just the practical side of what trees can do.

Trees are also beautiful to look at! Gaze up into the leafy canopy of a large old tree. You'll know right away why trees have inspired poets and songmakers since time began. Put your arms around a tree, and you will feel its strength and dignity.

When you plant a tree, and care for it, you are adding that beauty and strength to the world. You'll be helping people and nature at the same time, too.

A baby seedling

Every tree begins its life as a tiny seedling. A young seedling looks like a small stick, with just a few twigs and leaves on it. Yet that same seedling will grow into a stately, dignified, adult tree! Properly cared for, it will be there for your grandkids to play under! That's a lot of shade on hot days, and bird songs in spring. And you can start it all today!

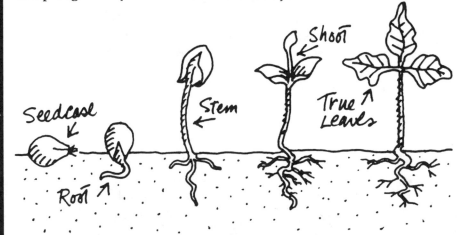

TO PLANT A TREE

Tree planting is really as simple as one, two, three—if you follow a few basic principles.

1 While you are waiting to plant your tree, make sure its roots are kept moist and that the seedling is not exposed to the hot sun. If the roots of the tree are not wrapped, place the seedling in a bucket of water in a shady place until you're ready to plant. Then, start digging a big hole, big enough to hold the roots of the tree.

Some trees come with their roots wrapped up in balls of burlap. Ask the person who gave you the tree if the ball is biodegradable. If it is, you can simply plant the tree, burlap and all.

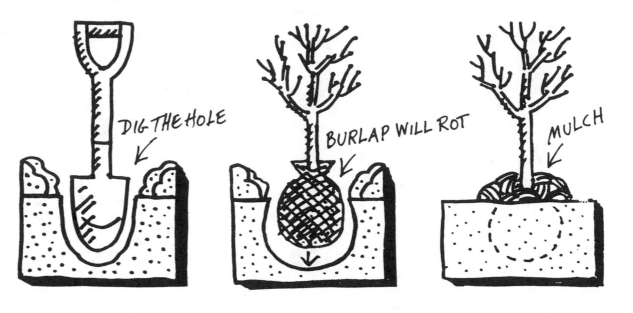

DIG THE HOLE

BURLAP WILL ROT

MULCH

2 When you've got the hole prepared, pour some water into it before you put the tree in. This will give the tree an extra good drink on its first day. Then, set the tree into the hole, covering its roots with soil, filling in the hole, and packing the dirt down as you go.

It's best to avoid using fertilizer on a newly planted tree. Let that wait till next year. For food, put woodchips or leaves around the base of the tree, but not directly over the place where the trunk meets the earth. This is called *mulching*. The chips or leaves will break down, providing good food for your tree.

3 Many people like to have a ceremony after their tree is planted. You can talk to your tree and wish it good luck as it grows. You can dedicate your tree to wildlife. You can promise to take good care of the tree. Having your picture taken next to the tree will provide a wonderful souvenir of the tree-planting.

Actually, your tree won't need that much help from you once it's planted. Give it lots of water on the first day and over the next several weeks. Old bath water, soapy dishwashing water, water that vegetables were cooked in, are all fine.

After that, check on the tree from time to time. Make sure it has water, especially in the late fall. Many trees go thirsty then. Once a year, or so, add more mulch. An occasional word of encouragement never hurts either!

A year from now, go to the tree for another picture. Wow! How you'll both have grown!

DETOX YOUR HOUSE

Is your house friendly? Evironmentally friendly, that is. You can find out by asking your home to take this little test. (If your house has trouble reading and writing, just take it for her.)

True or false

1. I stay bug- and weed-free by using lots of pesticides.

2. I need and use lots of heat to stay real hot in the winter.

3. My air-conditioning runs all day long in the summer.

4. I use strong chemicals to get clean inside.

5. I have a drippy faucet.

6. I don't have a recycling center, because no one ever set one up for me.

7. I love paper plates in my kitchen, and I use them whenever I can.

8. I have paper towels for picking up every little spill.

If your house would answer "true" to any of those statements, then it definitely isn't as friendly as it should be!

Pesticides are killers

Pesticides don't just kill weeds — they also pollute water, and sometimes harm innocent birds, and insects!

In the old days, people thought that dusting every living thing with chemicals would kill only unwanted bugs or weeds and let the others flourish. But water pollution, endangered species, people's illnesses, and more pest invasions taught us the truth. Pesticides made more problems than they solved.

The "lawn" around an environmentally friendly house may not always look picture perfect. It doesn't mind a few low-growing weeds, like chickweed, if they help feed the local birds. Some environmentally friendly homes have even changed their lawns into rock gardens, or into meadows with low-growing plants. (See Make a Nature Preserve, page 18.)

ENERGY WASTE HURTS EVERYBODY

When it comes to the environment, every little bit helps — or harms. Putting on a sweater instead of turning up the heat may not sound like much, but it's actually a heroic act as far as Planet Earth is concerned. Unfortunately, the oil, gas, and nuclear energy we use to heat our homes all make pollution. Until people figure out how to make non-polluting energy, we should use energy wisely. That means blocking drafts in the winter and going easy on air-conditioning in the summer.

Make a draft-eating snake

Turn a pillowcase inside out and cut a strip about 6" (15 cm) down the case. Be sure to cut through both pieces of cloth. Sew up the long end, so you have a long, skinny bag. Turn the bag right side out and fill it with sand or sawdust. Then sew the top shut.

Now, using fabric paint, or any kind of acrylic paint, decorate the pillowcase with snake markings — stripes, dots, or triangles. Add buttons for eyes, and yarn for a tongue.

Put the snake across the bottom of a door or windowsill. He will guard your house from drafts, and help to save energy!

STRONG CHEMICAL CLEANERS HURT LAND, AIR AND WATER

Some of the substances sold for cleaning are more toxic than they need to be! Harmful cleaners don't clean any better than environmentally friendly ones, either! Know which is which. For instance, avoid using ammonia — breathing it can hurt your lungs. Most jobs that ammonia can do, can be done just as well with some lemon juice or vinegar mixed with water.

Homemade cleaning power

You can make your own cleaning substances that will do just as well as those which pollute the air, ground or water. Simple, homemade cleaners are good for your family's pocketbook, too, since they don't cost much to make.

Window cleaner. Put ¹/₂ water and ¹/₂ white vinegar in a re-used spray bottle.

Dishwashing "detergent." Use liquid or powdered soap, such as Ivory, with 1 teaspoon (5 ml) of white vinegar or lemon juice per bottle. Real detergents are bad for water and especially for fish.

Disinfectants. Mix ¹/₄ cup (50 ml) of borax into a half gallon (1.87 L) of hot water. Even hospitals are starting to use borax to kill germs.

Oven cleaner. Make a paste of baking soda and water. Slather it on the oven walls, let it sit five minutes, and then scrub it off.

Household spray cleaner. One part strained lemon juice to six parts water. Smells nice, too!

Instead of mothballs, use cedar chips. They keep moths away and smell good, too!

• Even the way you eat helps or hurts the planet. It takes over 5,000 gallons (18.75 KL) of water to make 1 pound (.5 kg) of beef, but only 24 gallons (90 L) to grow 1 pound (.5 kg) of potatoes!

• Here's a saying to live by: *Use it up, Wear it out, Make it do, or Do without!*

NEIGHBORHOOD RECYCLING INC.

You can make money by recycling!

If you live in a state with a bottle return law, you can get money for every empty can or bottle you bring back to the store.

Now, you may not be able to buy much with the money your family makes returning bottles, but think about this: What if all the cans and bottles in the neighborhood were collected and returned, with the refund going to a worthy cause? It could be a neighborhood basketball hoop, or money for a block party, or a donation to charity.

If your state doesn't have a bottle return law, you can *still* make money recycling. Look under "Recycling" or "Resource Recovery" in the yellow pages. There you will find companies in the business of turning trash into useful stuff. With a little organization, you and your neighbors can benefit in a very direct way by selling to these companies.

Give the eldery a hand with recycling

Recycling can be hard for some old people, especially those who are not in the best of health. If there's someone like that in your neighborhood, and if you're old enough, you can help! Why not volunteer to carry bundles of papers and other reuseable items out of the house for the elderly person you know?

S.O.S.

IT'S AN EMERGENCY! Your planet really needs you, and other kids, to help turn some mighty big environmental problems around. Here's a list of groups that are already working to help. You can write to them for more information and they will write back. Get involved this weekend!

Center for Marine Conservation
(address on page 143)

National Wildlife Federation
(address on page 21)

The Nature Conservancy International
(address on page 146)

World Resources Institute
1709 New York Ave. NW
Washington, DC 20006

National Coalition Against the Misuse of Pesticides
701 E. St. SE, Suite 200
Washington, DC 20036

People for the Ethical Treatment of Animals (PETA)
PO Box 42516
Washington, DC 20015-0516

Renew America
1400 Sixteenth St. NW, Suite 710
Washington, DC 20036
(They keep a record of environmental successes! Maybe a project you create or work on can be listed.)

In Canada contact:

**Friends of the Earth
(Les Amis de la Terre)**
47 Clarendon St., Suite 306
Ottawa, Ontario K1N 9K1

Canadian Environmental Network
945 Wellington St., Suite 300
Ottawa, Ontario K1Y 2X5

Pollution Probe
12 Madison Avenue
Toronto, Ontario M5R 2S1

"WHAT HAS BEEN SPOILED THROUGH MAN'S FAULT CAN BE MADE GOOD AGAIN THROUGH MAN'S WORK"

— I Ching

BACK TO NATURE

Make a Nature Preserve

Do you love to hear birds singing? Does the sight of a rabbit hopping by make you smile? Well, even if your backyard is the size of a postage stamp, you can still turn it into an important miniature nature preserve. By making your corner of the world a safe haven for wildlife, you'll become part of a rescue mission that's helping save Planet Earth from ecological disaster — and you can have fun at the same time!

LOOK & LISTEN — IS ANYBODY HOME?

Chances are you've already got wildlife living close by — probably more kinds than you realize! Wrens, sparrows, squirrels, chipmunks, raccoons, snails, moles, butterflies, bees, bats, and rabbits are just a few of the wild creatures who often live close to people.

Look out your window, and visit your backyard at odd times of day. Take along a notebook and pencil and see how many creatures you can spot. Wild creatures are masters of *camouflage*. They are often much closer to you than you imagine, but well hidden from view.

Finding evidence of other backyard inhabitants requires a little more detective work. If it's winter, did you see animal tracks in the early morning snow? Has your garbage ever been tipped over during the night? If so, it was probably the work of raccoons rummaging for a free handout. Your nose will tell you if skunks live nearby.

Walk around any big trees. Are there nests overhead? Are there small holes by the roots? Maybe you're looking at a rabbit's hutch or chipmunk's house.

Write down all your findings, noting the season and year. This list of backyard inhabitants will serve as your "before" list.

SQUIRREL   RACCOON   RABBIT   MOUSE

Native American Nature Count

The first Americans kept count of what was important to them by marking hides and bark with feather pens and homemade dyes. You can make a Native American count of the animal life that shares your habitat with you by tearing the shape of a hide from a brown grocery bag.

Design symbols for the kinds of wildlife you've seen on your preserve. Write the approximate number of each kind of animal with a simple, small line. Store your count by rolling it up and tying it with a piece of dried corn husk or yarn.

PLAN AND PLOT

On a separate page in your notebook, draw a sketch of your property. Imagine that you are in a helicopter flying directly overhead. Draw what you'd see if you looked down.

Where there are large trees, put circles representing the trunks. For smaller trees, draw smaller circles. If you know the name of the trees, write them inside the circles. If you don't, pencil in a light question mark. When you've got all the trees on your map, draw in any hedges or bushes. Hedges can be squares or rectangles; bushes can be ovals. Follow these with different sized triangles to represent flowers and grasses. Fill in the names wherever you can. If you don't know the name of a particular plant or tree, ask around. Sometimes an older person might be able to help you make these identifications.

Markers and signs

It's not too early to start labeling what you've found. This way, visitors to your backyard preserve will have a better idea of what they're looking at. Begin by making markers for whatever trees and plants you've already identified. Later, as you come to know your plant life better, you can mark the others.

Markers can be made out of small, rectangular pieces of posterboard protected by transparent tape. Write down the name of the plant in bold letters with magic marker, and cover it securely with transparent, waterproof tape. Now your identifying sign is "laminated" so it'll be safe from the elements. Staple the marker onto a painted Popsicle stick and place it in the ground near the plant you have identified.

If you've found holes in the trees or the ground that are entrances to animals' homes, it's fun to mark them, too. (Examples: Mr. & Mrs. Squirrel, Chipmunk Manor, Look Up To See Bird's Nest.)

Now that you've done all you can with what's already there, it's time to roll up your sleeves and make some changes!

A wild spot

Creating a wild spot is ridiculously easy. Call it your reward for all the plotting and planning you've done. All you have to do is take a walk on the wild side, around your property. Look for a small spot that can simply be left alone. A small corner area near a fence or hedge is ideal.

Presto! By declaring this tiny plot of land forever wild, you've just given nature a great gift, something like a mini-grocery store. Here's why: Land that's left alone soon goes to seed. Make that birdseed. Most so-called "weeds" are really wildflowers that produce power foods for birds and other creatures. *A wild spot is like nature's pantry.*

To keep your wild spot healthy, cut down the stalks of the wild plants in late fall, after the plants have bloomed and turned brown. That's all there is to it.

PLANTING WITH A PURPOSE — YOU CAN IMPROVE ON NATURE

The best way to feed your local wild animals is to provide them with the berries, nuts, and fruits they thrive on, fresh off the vine, tree, and bush. To find out what food-bearing greenery is best for your area, talk to someone at your local nursery or to a neighbor who is experienced at feeding the birds.

When you know the kinds of plants that are best for attracting birds and other kinds of wildlife, send for some free gardening catalogues. Looking through a catalogue may inspire you with ideas for new plantings. It might help you to identify some of the mystery plants already growing on your preserve, too.

For free gardening catalogues contact: Burpee, Inc., 300 Park Ave., Warminster, PA 18974 (212-674-4915). Or, contact Farmer Seed and Nursery, Faribault, MN 55021 (507-334-1623).

UP, DOWN, ALL AROUND

Another key to a healthier habitat is having plants and trees of various heights. Some wild creatures nest and feed high up in trees. Others prefer life in bushes or on the ground. By making sure that your preserve includes green things of many different heights, you'll be able to accommodate more species.

Birds and small mammals, like rabbits, need hidden corridors and escape routes to flee from local predators. Look over your yard for good hiding places. Ordinary, creeping caterpillars, who will someday turn into brilliant butterflies, begin their lives hiding under dead leaves or loose pieces of bark.

If you need to create a good hiding place, try putting a couple of old logs, a used Christmas tree, or some fallen branches against a fence or hedge near your wild spot.

DINING AL FRESCO

Before you throw out old lettuce leaves, cucumber ends, and carrot shavings, think about this: a rabbit might consider them a delicious meal. How about leaving a corner of your garden as a compost heap/animal restaurant? It will help draw wildlife to your nature preserve and keep it there all year round.

A nature trail

If you've got some room to roam, try guiding visitors down the garden path, past all the signs you've made, past your butterfly garden and bird houses. Though you'll want to manicure the path itself, try to leave the rest of your nature trail as natural as possible. Dead trees, for instance, make great homes for animals, but only if you don't cut them down for firewood.

Making it official

Once you've got the fundamentals of your preserve in place, it's time to go for the gold! You can join the *National Wildlife Federation's Official Backyard Habitat Program* and receive official certification for the work you've done on behalf of your local wildlife. With your permission, the Federation will even contact your local paper to tell them about your accomplishment.

To receive an information packet with an official application and checklist, a how-to booklet, and 64-page book, send $12.95 to: Backyard Habitat Information Packet, *The National Wildlife Federation*, 8925 Leesburg Pike, Vienna, VA 22184. The fee is very reasonable and well worth the chance to be part of such an important program.

A CITY PRESERVE

Consider the many ways you can help wildlife in the city. Is your apartment building fringed with greenery? There may already be a bird's nest hidden in it, or perhaps a family of chipmunks live there. Check with the building manager or super about putting out a bird feeder in this common area. If you've done the leg work and can provide the materials, most supers will be happy to give permission for such a good cause.

A SIDEWALK GARDEN

Yes, it's true! You can grow a beautiful flower garden right in the crack of a sidewalk! All you need to do it is a skinny space between the concrete, an old fork, and a few seeds. Many sidewalks are not traveled enough to disturb a miniature garden, especially if you plant on the edges of the cement blocks.

What to plant

The best plants for a sidewalk garden are low-growing, hardy ones. Miniature Alyssum is a good choice, and so is a plant called Sedum. Both of these have tiny flowers. Alyssum blossoms are snow-white or purple and bloom all summer with just a little care.

Another good choice is Portulaca, with its showy bright flowers of orange and pink. (Birds like Portulaca, too, so you'll be encouraging your feathered friends to stop by the neighborhood when you plant it.)

If your sidewalk garden has a sunny spot near a drainpipe or a fence, try planting Morning Glory seeds. These climbing plants are very hardy. They grow fast and will reward your gardening efforts with many large flowers.

Getting started

Just like on a hundred-acre farm, you'll have to prepare the soil before you plant your sidewalk garden. Loosen the soil in the slit with a fork. If the dirt you're working with has been dried out and neglected for a long time, you may want to mix a couple handfuls of fresh potting soil in with it.

When the dirt is nice and crumbly, place seeds in it, one or two at a time, a few inches apart. Then cover the seeds with a little more soil, pat it all down, and give it a drink of water. Remember to be very gentle when you first water your sidewalk garden. You don't want to wash the tiny seeds away! A good method to use is the upside-down soda bottle technique. Fill a plastic bottle with water, cover the top loosely with your hand, turn the bottle upside down. As you shake out the water, it will come out like gentle rain. Your sidewalk garden will need to be watered fairly often, almost every day in very hot weather. Make sure the soil doesn't dry out for more than a day or two.

Success!

Keep watching and watering, and in a week to ten days, you'll see tiny seedlings pop out of the soil! That's a sign of success. Check your seedlings often and watch how they grow and change. In a few weeks, you'll have beautiful flowers growing right in the crack of the sidewalk!

FIRST AID FOR CITY TREES

Emergency! Emergency! Many city trees aren't getting the care they need to thrive! And when you think of all the nice things trees do for us, like keeping us cool by giving us shade, and keeping us healthy, by cleaning our air, then you'll surely want to rescue a city tree.

What's the problem?

City trees are fighting for their lives because it's hard for them to get what they need to live. Like all living creatures, trees need air, water, and food. Trees take these in by their roots. But if their roots are covered with concrete, or if the soil they're growing in has no nutrients, or if they don't get enough rainwater, a city tree could actually die! Of course, that won't happen if you and your friends are around! Because kids can actually save trees' lives!

Kids to the rescue: A tree needs you!

Find a pail or large container, something to dig with like a garden trowel, which is a hand-held shovel (an old spoon will do in a pinch), an old fork, work gloves (an old pair of winter ones is fine), and a litter bag.

You might want to talk to the tree as you work. Many people, including Native Americans, believe that trees can understand us, and even communicate back in their own silent way.

Help is on the way

A clean tree is a happy tree. Unfortunately, though, some careless people seem to confuse beautiful leafy trees with garbage pails! Yuck!

It's a good thing you're around, though. Get your gloves on and start your tree saving by clearing out any litter that's under the tree. You may find candy wrappers and cigarette filters, old coffee cups, and pop tab tops. The sooner you get rid of them, the happier your tree will be.

Make a litter picker-upper

If you hate handling litter, even with gloves on, you can make a litter picker-upper. All you need is a stick and a headless nail. Have a grown-up drive the nail into the end of the stick, and presto! You've got a professional litter picker-upper.

DOCTOR KID, REPORT IMMEDIATELY TO CITY SOIL SURGERY

Too often, the soil around a city tree has been neglected and abused so badly that it can't help the tree to live. You can help by reconditioning the soil to make it healthy again.

If the soil is tightly packed, it is not healthy for a tree. You can use an old fork, spoon, or garden trowel to gently dig up the top 2 or 3 inches (5 or 7.5 cm) of soil around your tree. (Don't dig deeper; it might hurt a root.) Digging up the top layer of soil will make it easier for the tree roots to take in air and water. Ahhh! What a relief!

Feed me! Love me! Hug me! Mulch me!

Once the soil is loosened it's time for a feeding. Woodchips, fallen leaves, some buried compost, peat moss, even composted manure can be sprinkled around the tree. Spreading this cover of natural materials over the soil is called mulching.

Mulching protects the tree during the winter. When the mulch breaks down by spring, it'll provide healthy food to the tree roots. Yum!

If you find earthworms in the park, you might want to bring them to your tree to put in the soil, too. Earthworms are the wonder workers of soil. Be sure to put enough worms in so that they will be able to mate. Six to ten should be enough.

Water me, please!

We all need water to live, and trees are no different. You can prevent a thirsty city tree from dying by tending to its water needs. Unless it has just rained, give the tree about six gallons of water, two times a week. Water in the late afternoon when the sun is down. Extra water is nice for a tree in the hot days of summer, but the really critical time is in the late fall. More city trees die of thirst in the fall than at any other time of year. But not *your* tree, of course!

HUG A TREE

Now that you've helped a tree to live, why not give it a big hug? If you do, you'll be sure to feel all the gratitude that big creature has to give. When you hug a tree you can feel the life inside it. Wrap your arms around it, and you'll get a dose of its special strength and power.

The tree you helped will be a faithful friend, too. Walking by and saying hello will connect you with nature in a new way. And if you're sad, go visit your tree. It's sure to give your spirits a lift!

Trees give back. Tree-mendously. Maybe they realize, even more than we do, just how much people and trees really need each other.

CHRISTMAS TREE PRESERVE

1. Find an old tree.

2. String it with berries, popcorn, seed balls, etc., for birds to eat.

3. Set it out in an inconspicuous place behind your building, or on the roof, if you are allowed.

4. Don't forget to hang some colored string on it in early spring. Your feathered friends will use it to build their nests!

A BIRD OASIS

You can have a nature preserve, even if you live in an apartment. A window feeder can be a welcome oasis for a hungry, tired bird who's come to town. With just a little planning and upkeep, your preserve can serve a vital purpose for migrant birds as well as local ones. Inexpensive, easy-to-attach window feeders are available from Duncraft (800-252-5696).

Providing water in a city preserve may be more difficult, but it's not impossible. If you have a window box, try submerging a small bowl and keeping it half-filled with clean water. Change the water every other day or so. Your bowl of water will be a miniature pond or lake. If it's more than two inches deep, set a stone in it as a bird perch.

During times of drought, it's a great favor to the birds if you collect rain water in a pan for them. A cake pan with a medium-sized stone for birds to perch on will do fine. That way, when rainwater puddles dry up, the water in your pan will save the day!

The plants you include in your window-box should be bird-attracting plants. Here are a few suggestions for windowbox flowers that please humans and birds alike: Zinnias, Marigolds, Verbena, Portulaca, Dwarf Asters, Bachelor Buttons, and Coreopsis (also known as Tickseed).

Your efforts will be well rewarded, too. Birds feeding outside your window brighten up any day!

Create a Bird Sanctuary

No nature preserve is complete without a plan for the care and feeding of birds. Songbirds have been hard hit by the forward march of civilization. Only people can save them from further destruction, and one way is by inviting them to share our space.

When you are enjoying the peaceful, green calm and the melodious birdsong that a backyard preserve offers, you may wonder who is doing whom the favor!

OPEN FOR BUSINESS • THE SONGBIRD CAFE •

Bird feeders are simple to make. Even something as simple as tossing bread crumbs onto the lawn will be appreciated by ground-feeding birds, such as crows. (Bread-crumb tossing is a good way to get toddlers involved with the preserve, too.) Some temporary feeders can be put up in only a few minutes.

To get you started, here are four of the world's easiest bird feeders to make. You can use them to tempt birds to your yard, while you plan more permanent structures.

The world's easiest bird feeders

Feeder A Place half of an overripe orange or grapefruit on a broken branch. Remove after two days.

Feeder B Sew a string of whole, unshelled peanuts onto a ribbon, and hang it on a tree.

Feeder C Smear a pine cone with peanut butter and roll it in bird seed. Hang from a tree.

Feeder D Sew a garland of popcorn and put it on a tree.

Cheap, cheap, cheap!

Luckily, birdseed is inexpensive. Mixed varieties and ready-made "seed bells" can be purchased at the local supermarket or garden center. Many birds love sunflower seeds (striped, black, hulled, or unhulled), fine cracked corn, white millet, and thistle.

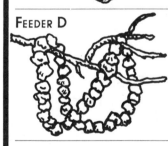

BIRDHOUSES AND BIRDBATHS

Whenever a shopping center is built on what was once woods, or a housing development replaces a meadow, the wild creatures who live there lose their homes. It's a tragedy — but one you can do something about.

The world's easiest birdhouse to make

Cut a 2½" (6 cm) entrance hole in a 6" to 8" (15 cm to 20 cm) orange and green gourd. Drill or whittle an opening for the bird, then scrape out the seeds. (You can whittle with a stone.) Drill or whittle a ½" (1 cm) drain hole at the bottom, and a ¼" (5 mm) hole through the top. Attach the gourd to a line and hang it in a tree. The house will last for one season.

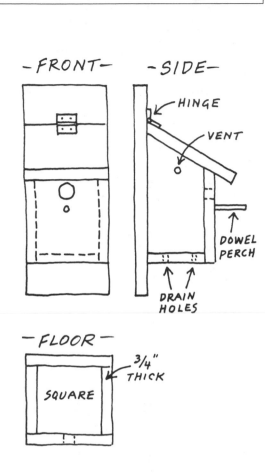

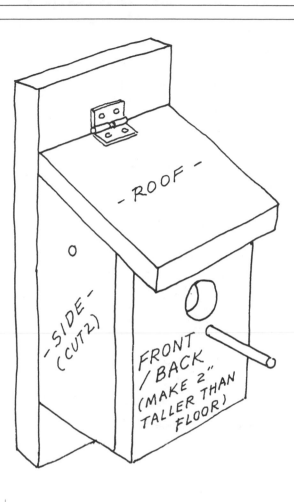

Basic birdhouse blueprint

Using this simple design, you'll be able to build a bird house in an afternoon.

Use cedar, pine, or cyprus wood, and brass or galvanized nails, if possible. Cut out the six pieces. Whittle or drill an entry hole. Drill holes on the bottom piece for drainage, and on the sides for ventilation. Attach the roof with a hinge or a piece of leather strapping.

The size of this house can be varied to attract different kinds of birds.

For chickadees, wrens, nuthatches, and titmice make the floor dimension 4" x 4" (10 cm x 10 cm). For bluebirds and tree swallows increase floor to 5" x 5" (12.5 cm x 12.5 cm); and for flycatchers and woodpeckers increase it to 6" x 6" (15 cm x 15 cm). (If you are hoping to attract chickadees, fill the house with woodshavings. Chickadees make their nests by digging them out.)

Other basic birdhouse designs are available from most hobby shops. They often carry inexpensive pre-cut birdhouse kits, too, that are ready for super quick assembly.

Home Sweet Tree

If you want to paint your birdhouse for better protection against the weather, remember that birds prefer the look of dull, weathered grays and browns. In fact, if a birdhouse is brightly painted, birds will avoid it! If you can find wood with the bark still on it, the birds will like it best of all.

Interior decoration for your feathered friends

In spring, put 3" to 4" (7.5 cm to 10 cm) pieces of colorful yarn and thread on trees for birds to use in building their nests. If you have an evergreen, you can decorate it like a Christmas tree. Another way to provide nesting material is to leave a basketful of nesting scraps in the middle of the lawn. If the timing is right, you may see bird mothers and fathers selecting their favorite bits while you watch from the window.

Birdhouse maintenance

When you're ready to place the birdhouses, remember to mount or hang them at varied heights on your property. For the basic birdhouse given here, elevate the house from 5' to 20' (2 m to 6 m). Late winter and early spring are the ideal times for putting the houses out. Avoid putting them in direct sunlight or anywhere that a cat can reach.

Later, when the occupants have flown south for the winter, take the house down and scrub it out. With care, your house will last for years.

AQUA VITAE

Whether for a sip or a dip, birds need water. An open, predator-safe birdbath is a vital part of any bird sanctuary. Without water, birds cannot survive. Providing water brings extra rewards, too. Many birds that shun feeders are happy guests at the birdbath.

Though birdbaths often sit on pedestals, many birds actually prefer bathing at ground level. That's probably because they use puddles for bathing in the wild.

The world's simplest birdbath

Place four bricks on the ground. Put an upside down metal garbage can lid on them. Make sure it doesn't wiggle. If you have permission, paint the inside deep blue or green. Fill the lid with water.

Make sure the water in your birdbath is no more than 2 or 3 inches (5 or 7.5 cm) deep. Replace water and sponge out the bath once a week.

Or try a *Frisbee birdbath* — just make three holes in the edge of a frisbee, run some string through the holes, hang it from the branch of a tree, and fill it with water!

water depth 2" to 3"

COUNTRY CLUB FOR BIRDS

Adding a pool to your property may sound like a major undertaking. But it's really very simple, if it's a miniature pool meant for birds.

First, pick out a space within reach of your garden hose. (That way, cleaning the pool will be easy.) Try to pick a spot that is in the open, so no maurauding cat can make an attack on the pool while the bathers are busy.

Next, choose a pleasing shape for the pool, one that can fit easily into an area of 2' x 3' (60 cm x 90 cm). You might want to experiment by putting a rope on the ground to find the shape you like best.

Now dig out the pool. Be sure it slopes very gently from just 1/2" (1 cm) to a depth of just four inches. Line the bottom with sand or small rocks. Gently press down a double thickness of heavy duty garbage bags on it. Hide the edges of the bags by covering them with dirt. Then put weighty and decorative stones around. Add a large stone to the deep end of the pool, for perching. Fill with water, and voila! A nature pool!

Syphon

One way to clean out your pool is with a syphon. It's easy to do, but you'll need some old hose or plastic tubing. Stick one end in the water, while covering the other end with your thumb, or have someone else help you. The end with your thumb should be placed lower than the end in the water. It helps if your pool is on slightly higher ground. The end in the water should be tilted to let air bubbles out and water in. Once the air is gone, release your thumb to get the water flowing out.

BACKYARD PRESERVE POOL

① Find the shape you like best

② Dig out a sloping hole

③ Cover with plastic

④ Line plastic-covered hole with small smooth stones

⑤ Cover edges with dirt

⑥ Edge pool with decorative rocks

⑦ Add large stone as perch

⑧ Fill with water

Unwanted guests

Occasionally you may find an unwanted guest in your nature preserve. Usually the offending party is a neighborhood cat or dog who thinks birds are better eaten than protected! In the case of an unruly pet, you can talk to the owner about limiting the pet's visits to your preserve.

Squirrels sometimes like to raid the local bird feeder, too, and they are not known for their good manners! Left to his own devices, a squirrel will eat every last grain of bird feed. Since they can hang upside down to feed, squirrels can be very clever about getting to the food, too.

Try to locate your feeders where squirrels can't get at them. Or, you might try putting out a device known as a squirrel baffler. These are large metal collars that hang over, or under a bird feeder. Another method of baffling squirrels is to coat the stand of a table-top feeder with a mixture of caulk and red cayenne pepper!

Some kind souls find that leaving an ear of corn out for the squirrels is the best way to handle the problem.

Don't expect overnight results

Now that your sanctuary is open for guests, remember that it may take time for visitors to find it. Little by little the wild creatures will show up, though, as they discover your helpful haven. Some will be migrants, stopping off as they travel across the globe. Others will come and take up residence. Just be patient while you're waiting for their arrival, and don't expect dramatic numbers. Birds especially are highly territorial. The ones who nest in your sanctuary may not want to share a good thing with others. They may actually drive others away! Take time to identify and get to know the creatures who share your space. While you're at it, you'll be enjoying the simple pleasure of the sanctuary you created.

Experts say there's been a fifty percent reduction in America's songbird population during the past hundred years.

Birds that like bushes: cardinals, mockingbirds, sparrows, warblers

Thomas Jefferson kept a nature notebook.

A high bush blueberry plant attracts 90 different species of birds!

I value my garden more for being full of blackbirds than cherries, and very frankly give them fruits for their songs.

Joseph Addison

People food that many birds like: popcorn, peanuts, apples, raisins.

FEELING SPECIAL

The Book of Me

CALLING ALL HEROES AND HEROINES

Have you ever dreamed of being the star of an exciting book? What book? Why, *The Book of Me!*

Autobiography

That's what it's called. An autobiography is the story of a person's life, written by that person. And while your autobiography may not make the bestseller list, it'll definitely be a lasting treasure for you and your loved ones. (In fact, you might all want to try writing one.)

You don't have to be a great author to write your book. After all, who knows more about your life than you? You know exactly which things have been important to you, and how you felt about them. You know the people, the places, and the events that have made your life what it is. You know what interests you, and what your dreams are.

Begin at the beginning — whenever that was!

It's funny. Everybody's life begins more or less the same way, yet each birth is unique. Aside from you and your mom, *who* was there? *Where* were you born? In what town? In a hospital? At home? In a cab? *What* did you look like? What did people say about you? (Answer all those questions, and you'll soon have Chapter One!)

Another place to begin your story is with your very first memories. Think back to when you were really little. Can you remember having a strong feeling about something? Do you remember something that made you happy? Sad? Confused? Even if it's not *exactly* the way it happened, a remembered event is a good jump-off point for an autobiography.

How long a book?

The chapters in your book don't have to be long. They can range from just three sentences to three pages, or more, if you're really inspired. As for the number of chapters, it's up to you, but most books have at least five.

Three different styles

A good start might go something like this:

"The great 'Me' was born on September 3, 1985. What a day! Not a cloud in the sky. The birds were singing about the new arrival, and how perfectly wonderful she was. `I've heard they named her Heather!' said Mrs. Robin to Mrs. Sparrow."

Or you might take a more hard-hitting approach:

"Stop the presses! There's big news today. As of seven o'clock this morning, there's a new fair-haired boy in the Holmes' household. His name is Raymond, and is he ever big! At nine pounds, nine ounces, he really came out fighting — fighting mad, that is. His parents said he cried for a solid hour . . ."

Here's another approach:

"The first thing I remember is when I dumped a spoon of tuna on the cat. I didn't want to hurt him. I just wanted to see what would happen. He liked it! That taught me to keep trying new things."

Sample chapter headings

Here are some chapter titles that may inspire you:

The New Arrival

Meet the Family

My Best Friends

School Days

Places I've Visited

Where I Used to Live

What I Like to Do

My Biggest Dream

My Most Embarrassing Moments

My Philosophy

The Best Thing that Ever Happened to Me

When I Grow Up

If I Ruled the World

PLAYS AND POETRY

The examples we gave so far, like most autobiographies, are written in *narrative* style. But you can choose to write *The Book of Me* in a very different form, too, like a *play* or a *poem*.

The Story of My Life — an autobiographical play

Plays are for reading as well as performing, and they can be fun to write. When you write a play, you don't write chapters, paragraphs, or even sentences. Instead, you write *acts* and *scenes*, with characters and settings. In a play, when people talk, it's called *dialogue*.

On the page, it looks something like this:

The Story of My Life
by Me

Act One, Scene One

Characters: A baby, a woman, and a man

Setting: A hospital room

Man: He looks just like me!

Woman: He does have a big nose.

Baby: Wahhhh!

Woman: But he's still the most beautiful baby!

Baby: Coo, coo...

Man: Did you hear that? He said, "Da-da!"

Scene Two

Woman and Baby

A living room

Woman: No, baby! Don't touch the fish food! Baby! Stop!

Baby: Yum! Yum!

The Epic of Me, a collection of poems

Look over the chapter heading ideas. What if they were poems? Try writing the story of your life as a poem, or group of poems. Like this:

The New Arrival

One fine Tuesday I was born,
At four A.M. on a stormy morn.
My mother said, "Oh, what a joy!
A six-pound, nine-ounce baby boy!"

and so on . . . .

KEEPING A JOURNAL

Writing in a journal or diary can be good for a person's soul. You can use a journal to express exactly what you think and feel. A journal can be private. You don't have to show it to other people until and unless you feel like it.

A journal is a treasure that becomes more valuable the older it is. If you read something you wrote a month or a year ago, you will learn a lot about yourself and how you've changed and grown.

But here's a warning: Even if you don't like what you've written in your journal, don't throw it out. The books and journals you're creating today will be more and more fascinating as years go by. Some things seem to get better with age. A statement you may find embarrassing now may make you smile appreciatively ten years from now!

The world of writing is a world of discovery

You can make up stories, too. You can invent imaginary places, people, and events out of your head and write it all down. Made-up writing is called *fiction*. Books that are long, made-up stories are called *novels*.

If you know a lot about a subject, you can write about that, too. Writing about factual things is called *non-fiction*.

The hardest part of writing

Ask any author, and they will tell you the same thing: the hardest part of writing is getting started. Some people find it difficult to face an empty sheet of paper. Suddenly, it seems to them that they haven't got one idea in their heads! That uncomfortable feeling is known as *writer's block*. Fortunately, there's an easy cure — *writing*!

If you're still having a horrible time getting started, try this old writer's trick: pretend you are writing a letter to someone you like. Just don't write "Dear So and So" at the top.

MAKING YOUR BOOK

Now that you've written your book — autobiography, story, novel, play, collection of poems or whatever — it's time to publish it!

You can even illustrate the book — with photos, copies of photos, pictures cut from magazines, or your own drawings. Certain souvenirs go well in books, too. Ticket stubs, programs, invitations, and cards, all make nice additions to scrapbooks.

Making a book by hand

The simplest book to make by hand is a stapled book. For this, you put the pages of the book in between two covers, and staple everything on the left side. A young child can put together a stapled book very quickly and easily.

You can improve a stapled book by adding a strip of decoration to cover the staples. Try a piece of lace, a strip of colored paper, or even wide, cloth, adhesive tape.

A hand-sewn book

A hand-sewn book will be a treasure for years to come. Its pages lie flat, and it can hold more pages than a stapled book.

To sew a book, use thick paper and extra strong thread. The paper should be twice as long as you want each page to be.

Put the pages together and fold them in half. Now open the book and mark a straight line in the middle in neat dots, about an inch (2.5 cm) apart. When you sew along the line, you've got a simple, hand-sewn book. As with the stapled book, you can cover the edge with lace, trimming, or cloth tape.

A cover to be proud of

If you've worked hard making your book, it certainly deserves a beautiful cover!

You can decorate the cover of your book with pictures you've drawn or cut from magazines, or with potato stamps.

Or you can make a simple flap cover. Fold the flaps of a long, strong piece of paper onto the inside of the book. (Make sure the book closes properly before you glue the flaps.)

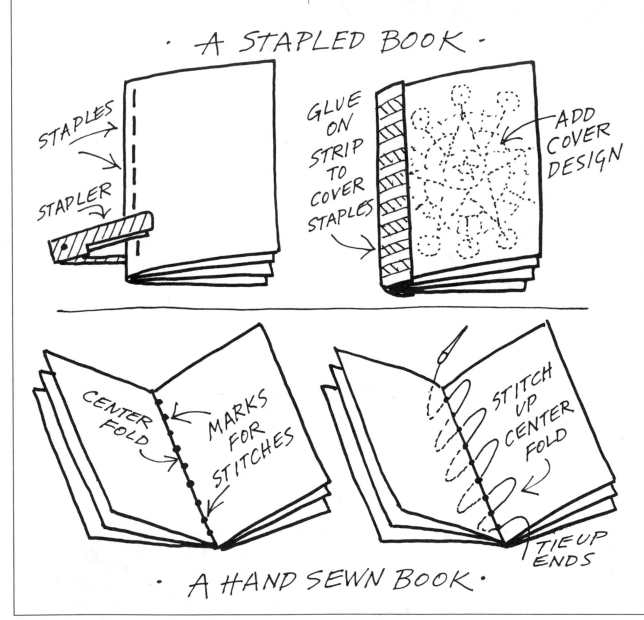

· A STAPLED BOOK ·

STAPLES

STAPLER

GLUE ON STRIP TO COVER STAPLES

ADD COVER DESIGN

CENTER FOLD

MARKS FOR STITCHES

STITCH UP CENTER FOLD

TIE UP ENDS

· A HAND SEWN BOOK ·

The ultimate — your own hard-covered book

A sturdy hard cover isn't as difficult to make as you might think. And the results are amazing.

You'll need two strong pieces of cardboard that are larger than the pages of your book. You will cover the two cardboards in exactly the same way.

Place the cardboard down onto the back of the material you want for the cover of your book. It can be gift wrap, road map, or even fabric — as long as you like it a lot.

Leaving an edge of about an inch (2.5 cm) on three sides, glue the cover material to what will be the front cover of your book. Fold over the edge and glue it down, snipping off two corners.

Hide the exposed cardboard on the inside covers by glueing paper over it.

When you've done both covers, front and back, in and out, you are ready to attach them.

Use cloth tape in the widest size. If you don't have tape, use strong cloth and glue. Attach the covers to the tape, leaving a half an inch (1 cm) or more in the middle where the pages will fit.

Place the whole construction under a heavy, flat object to dry. When it's ready, you can sew the pages into the cover.

A hand-sewn, hard-covered book is one of the best treasures ever. It's one of the classiest gifts you can make, too.

Writing must be dangerous! Professional writers call the beginning of a story the *point of attack*. The day they have to turn the story in is called a *deadline*. When they get paid for a story that doesn't get published, they get a *kill fee*. And if the book is a smash hit, they call it a *blockbuster*!

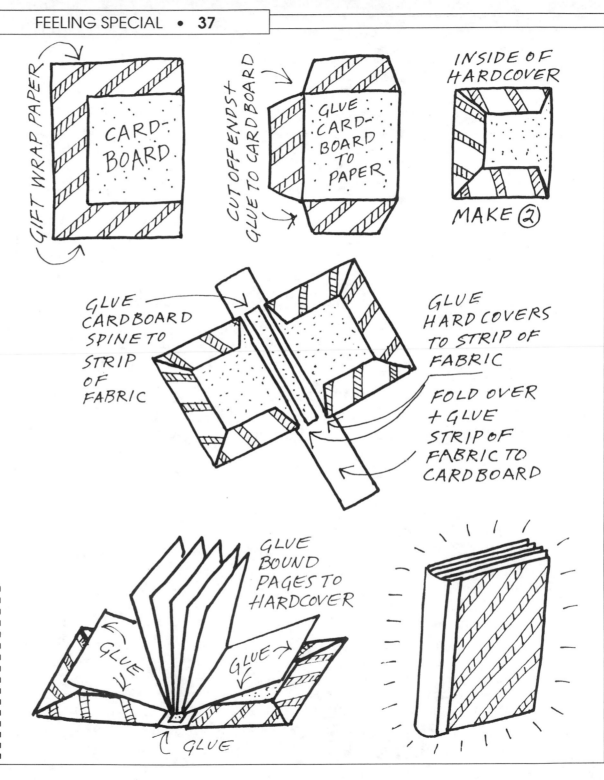

GIFT WRAP PAPER

CARD-BOARD.

CUT OFF ENDS + GLUE TO CARDBOARD

GLUE CARD-BOARD TO PAPER

INSIDE OF HARDCOVER

MAKE ②

GLUE CARDBOARD SPINE TO STRIP OF FABRIC

GLUE HARD COVERS TO STRIP OF FABRIC

FOLD OVER + GLUE STRIP OF FABRIC TO CARDBOARD

GLUE BOUND PAGES TO HARDCOVER

GLUE

GLUE

GLUE

SEAL OF · AFFECTION

PARENT APPRECIATION DAY

One of the best feelings parents ever experience is the feeling that their child appreciates them — not just on Mother's Day or Father's Day, and not just because the parent buys something special.

So if you do something nice for your parents as a complete *surprise*, it's sure to give them a big dose of that very special and wonderful feeling. Why not show them that you care on a day when they least expect it? It'll be fun to see their stunned reaction.

SUNDAY MORNING BREAKFAST IN BED

The secret of a successful breakfast in bed is being up before the person who's receiving the breakfast. Set your alarm extra early, so you have plenty of time to prepare the surprise. And while you're getting the breakfast together try to be as quiet as possible. You don't want to wake your unsuspecting parent with clattering dishes before the surprise is ready.

MAKE SOMEONE HAPPY

You'll need a tray

The tray — and how you set and serve it — is far more important than what food is on it! Look for a small vase to put a fresh flower or a couple of leaves in. Use the best china, with a cloth napkin, if possible.

The breakfast fare

A toasted English or any kind of muffin is perfect, with a piece of fresh fruit. A small pot of tea or hot chocolate completes the breakfast. If your parent is a coffee drinker, coffee is a must. If you don't know how to make it, ask another grown-up to help.

If your parent likes to read the morning newspaper, bring that to him, too.

Two sample menus

Menu #1

Toasted English muffin with slices of orange
Pot of chamomile tea

Menu #2

Lemon scones* with fresh strawberries
Pot of hot chocolate

*For recipe, see Tea Party, page 49.

Good morning!

When the time comes, knock lightly on your parent's door, and announce, "Breakfast has arrived!" Wish her a good morning and hand her the tray; then slip out of the room with a smile. Your mother (or father) may be floored, but she'll sure be happy!

SHOWING THAT YOU CARE

There are lots of ways that kids can show their parents they care. How about shining all of Dad's shoes for him? If you don't already do it regularly, try handling a load of laundry or two. Remember to sort the whites, the lights, and the darks from each other. Won't Mom be pleased and surprised when she gets home!

Or you can make your parent a gift. Store-bought gifts are nice, but handmade ones are fantastic (see Classy Gifts to Make, page 154).

And how about leaving your mom or dad a nice note? Put it where they'll be sure to find it, like on their pillow. Letting them know that you love them is one of the best gifts a kid can give!

Shoe shining

You'll need polish, and a newspaper, and possibly a shoe brush and a rag.

Put the shoes that need polishing on newspaper to avoid a mess. Wipe the shoes with a damp rag, before you apply the polish. Make sure you are using the right color for the shoe you're shining.

When the polish has dried, rub the shoe with a clean, dry rag or an old pair of mom's nylon stockings. That will make it extra shiny.

(If you don't have shoe polish, use the inside of a fresh banana peel! Rub the peel over the shoe, and you'll get a terrific, if temporary, shine.)

An unbirthday

Want to give someone a nice surprise? Wish them a Happy *Un*birthday, and then give them a special treat, like a gift or a cupcake! Unbirthdays are great if you like someone but don't know when his or her real birthday is, too.

MAKE A GIFT BASKET

Is there a shut-in on your block? An older person who can't get out much? Someone who isn't feeling well and has to stay in bed?

Well, you can cheer that person up in a hurry! Just make him a gift basket and deliver it in person!

Start with the basket itself. Most families have some extras lying around from the last time flowers or a basket of fruit was delivered. If not, inexpensive baskets can be bought at garden or houseware stores. Or, you can make a container by decorating something you find around the house, like an old shoebox or coffee can.

Now — what to put in the basket? Well, start by thinking what that special person might like to have. Would fruit be good? Some tea bags? How about a work of art you made yourself? Or a caring card you designed at home? A picture of you or your family or just of something funny?

Now deliver your basket. Ring the person's doorbell, and when he answers, blow on a trumpet or kazoo, and yell, "Surprise!" Or pretend you're the postman and say "Special delivery!" Or just leave your basket at the door and hide behind a nearby bush or tree. That way, you can spy on the person as he or she gets your delightful surprise!

There's nothing that makes you feel quite as special as doing something nice for somebody else.

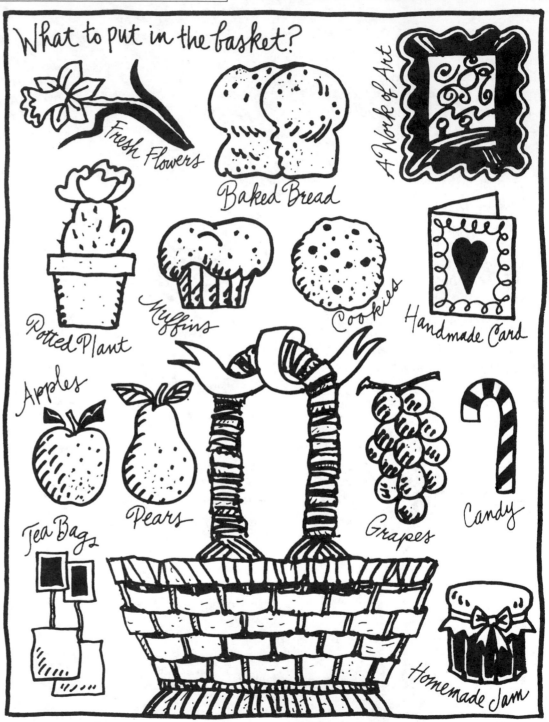

What to put in the basket?

Fresh Flowers • Baked Bread • A Work of Art • Potted Plant • Muffins • Cookies • Handmade Card • Apples • Pears • Tea Bags • Grapes • Candy • Homemade Jam

SILENT TIME

This quiet time activity is really quiet! So quiet that you may wonder where everyone has gone, if they aren't in the same room with you. All you have to do is stay silent for an agreed upon period of time, whether it's a whole day, an hour, or ten minutes.

> *The only rule is: no words. When you need to "say" something, you can use any other means but speech.*

Taking time to be silent may sound easy, but it's not. In fact, most people find it incredibly challenging — and just as fascinating, too.

By yourself, or with others

Silent Time can be done by one person or by the whole family. If you're doing it on your own, it's important to tell people about it before you begin. Otherwise, the rest of the family may be baffled, wondering what strange disease has left you looking so healthy, yet acting so speechless!

Once everyone has been informed about what's going on it's time to shush. Aah, how peaceful when quiet descends on the house. That is, until you need to tell somebody something.

Communicating without words

Ironically, Silent Time is a wonderful exercise in self-expression. Because even when you are being silent, you will still have to communicate.

If you want to express love during silent time, try a hug. If you want to argue, you'll have to do it in body language, which makes for some pretty funny disagreements. If you want to be friendly, smile or pat someone on the shoulder.

OTHER WAYS OF COMMUNICATING

Your hands, face, and body provide a way to express yourself. You'll be surprised at how much you can communicate without words, though you may fumble around a bit, too.

That's when some simple hand, head, and facial gestures will come to the rescue. Some of them you already use — like shaking your head up and down for "yes," and sideways for "no."

SIGN LANGUAGE

American Indians used hand language when they had meetings of tribes that spoke different languages. Today, deaf and hearing-impaired persons use hand language, too. Their language, called *American Sign Language*, is amazingly complete — and beautiful, too.

Some people can even "sing" in this silent language, to pre-recorded music. The words of the song are "signed" with expressive movements of hands, face, and body. As an art form, silent singing is extremely expressive and moving. Why don't you try signing one of your favorite songs? There is a dictionary of sign language in most libraries that will tell you any word you don't know. You can perform your song at the end of Silent Time as a kind of celebration.

How to "speak" by signing

Some American Sign Language is taken from the everyday movements people make. For instance, to say "I," simply point to yourself. To say "you," point to the person you're signing to.

Facial expressions are part of this language, too. For instance, the sign for "I understand" is the same as for "I don't understand." The difference is the look on your face when you make the sign!

Try these simple phrases in sign. How many different things can you say?

AMERICAN SIGN LANGUAGE ALPHABET

In ASL, people sign and spell. Here is the ASL alphabet. Can you learn to spell your name? With practice, how quickly can you spell it?

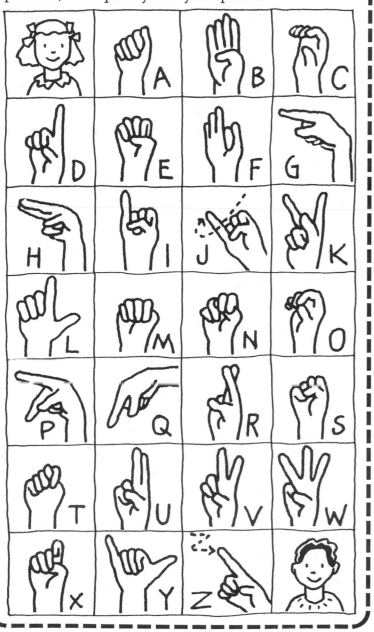

Mime

Mime is another delightful way to communicate. Describe something by acting it out, or tell a story. You can even act out your own "Silent Movie." If more than one person is sharing Silent Time, you can all act out a story you know or make one up. It's amazing how much can be communicated without words, once you put your mind to it.

SILENCE IS GOLDEN

Take a good listen to the silence around you. Not so silent, is it? In fact, the world around us is a pretty noisy place!

Many of these sounds are there all the time, but we don't hear them because we're so busy making noise of our own. Silent Time helps us to listen and get to know our world in a whole new way.

As you go soundlessly through your day's activities, you'll find yourself settling into the silence. On a walk, or reading a book, a cozy sense of inner harmony may come over you. You'll find there's something deep and wonderful about the sounds of silence as you listen to the life around you, and quietly take it all in. Many people feel renewed and relaxed after a Silent Time. You may learn first-hand why ancient wisdom tells us that *silence is golden*.

The National Theatre of the Deaf is a theatre company which puts on performances of classic and modern plays, all in sign language! They sometimes tour the country, so maybe you'll be lucky enough to catch one of their performances. You can find out more about them by calling their information number or writing for information.

National Theatre of the Deaf
PO Box 659
Chester, CT 06412

Telephone: 860-526-4971
860-526-4974
(tdd – for special hearing devices)

FAMILY TREE

When you say the word "family," what do you think of? Your mother and father, sister and brother? Did you include your grandparents? What about all those aunts, uncles, cousins, nieces, nephews, and assorted "distant relatives"? Do you have any "in-laws" or "relatives by marriage"?

Before you know it, your family, which started out at a very manageable number, has gotten way out of hand.

But you can keep track of it — with a family tree. Not only will you be able to see, at a glance, just how all your relatives are related to you, you'll have a much better idea of your heritage — where and who you came from.

That's right — your family tree doesn't just include members who are alive today. Just like a real tree, it has roots, along with branches and blossoms.

HOW TO BEGIN

Go to your mother and father, or to your aunts and uncles, and grandparents, grandaunts and uncles, if they're around. Bring a tape recorder with you, to capture any fascinating stories about the old days.

Ask them about their parents, their grandparents, even their great-grandparents, if they can remember back that far. Don't just ask for names. Ask them to tell you everything they remember about their ancestors — hair color, eye color, height, and weight, for example. Did they have any special talents, such as a good sense of humor, musical or artistic ability? What did they do for a living? Where did they come from? What year were they born? When did they die, and what did they die of? Find out about who they married, and all about their children. And *write it all down.*

We each have two parents, four grandparents, eight great-grandparents, and so on, back as far as people's memories can take you. When you've gone as far back as you can go, you've reached the roots of your family tree.

Making your tree

Now, it's time to lay out your chart. The first thing to know is that a family tree has the roots on top — it's upside down, with you at the bottom.

Let's say, for example, that you were able to go back as far as your great-grandparents (there are eight of these, remember). We'll start with just one and follow her down.

A sample tree

We'll call our great-grandmother "A," and draw a box for her at the top of our chart.

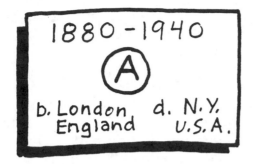

The dates say that "A" was born in 1880 and died in 1940. The places say that she was born in London, England and died in New York City, U.S.A. If you know other things about her, make the box bigger and add them in. If you have a picture, put it in, too, or make a photocopy and use that. Pictures will make your family tree really come alive.

Okay, let's say we're done with great-grandmother A. Now it's time to connect her with great-grandfather B.

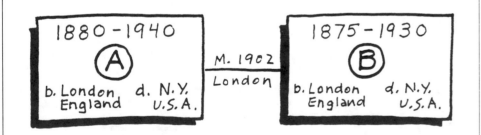

This box tells when and where "B" was born and died. The line between them tells when and where they were married — in London, in 1902.

Now let's say A and B had children — three of them. We'll call them "C," "D," and "E." Let's say C and D got married and had children of their own.

The third child, E, had no children. Now our chart would look something like this:

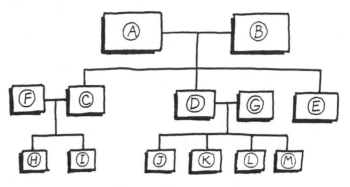

Notice that we've called C's husband "F," and D's wife "G." We've named their children "H," "I," "J," "K," "L," and "M." Let's say C is your grandmother and F is your grandfather. H is your mother, and I is your uncle — your mom's brother.

Now we've extended the chart another generation. "N" is your dad. "R" is you, and "S" is your brother. "O" is your aunt, and "T" is your first cousin.

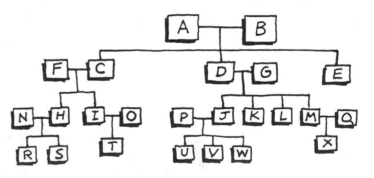

We could go on, but by now you get the picture. Everybody's family tree is different and unique. The more information you can fit in the boxes, the more complete and interesting a picture you'll have of where you come from, and how you fit into the big picture of your family.

If someone is still alive, mark it like this: 1940-
(Leave the date of death blank.)

People on the same level across from one another are in the same "generation" — brothers, sisters, and cousins.

LOOKING AT YOUR TREE

You'll notice, first of all, how enormous your tree soon becomes — remember, we've only traced *our* tree from two great-grandparents. Imagine if we'd included all eight! Or if our tree went even further back, or if there were more children along the way, or second marriages! Remember to use a big piece of cardboard or posterboard for the final version of your tree. You'll need it!

Now it's time to study the chart you've made, to see what you can learn from it. Did you notice which different countries your ancestors came from? How many generations of your family have lived in this country? Most of our ancestors came from elsewhere, and settled here to find a better life.

GENETICS AND HERITAGE

Notice other things, too. Do you, or your siblings, share some of the same traits as your cousins or ancestors? Are you left-handed like your great-grandfather? Are you musical like Grandma Jane?

Red-headed like Great-uncle Charlie? You'll probably find that you have certain things in common with many other members of your family tree. This shouldn't surprise you — after all, not only do you share a heritage, you also share many of the same *genes*.

The science of genetics was invented by a botanist named Gregor Mendel. He discovered that plants could be crossed with each other to create offspring that had traits of both. He found out that traits can come from the ancestors of both the mother and the father. Sometimes these traits are hidden for a generation or two, only to reappear in grandchildren or great-grandchildren. Is this true in your family tree?

What if you're adopted?

If you're adopted, then you've been grafted onto the family tree! Farmers and tree experts use grafting to make the sweetest fruits in the best new varieties. In the same way, you add new life to the family tree you've become a part of.

Tea Time

What's more fun than an old-fashioned tea party? Indoors or out, this time-honored activity is sure to please everyone, kids and grown-ups alike. From the preparation of the brew to the very last sip, a tea party seems to bring out the best in us. It is terribly civilized, and a great excuse to practice good manners — to say nothing of phony British accents.

There's nothing like a made-up English accent to get your tea party off to a good start. Liberal use of phrases such as "I say," "pip, pip," and "jolly good" are highly recommended. You might even want to give yourself a noble title for the occasion, such as Lord So and So, Lady This and That, or the Baroness of _____ Street (fill in yours).

What you'll need

The only essentials are decaffeinated tea, milk, lemon, and sugar, a few cookies, and, of course, guests. While you're at it, remember to invite your imagination. This is the perfect time to bring out a carton of dress-up clothes, with as much costume jewelry as possible. Fancy dress and lipstick for the ladies, Dad's old suit jacket and eyebrow-pencil moustaches for the gentlemen are recommended.

A tablecloth is a must; a clean towel will substitute nicely if none is handy. To grace the table, a sprig of flowers or leaves will serve quite well.

Who to invite

Everyone enjoys a tea party, but it's best to limit your guests to five or fewer if you have only one teapot. Older people will enjoy an invitation to this kind of get-together, so it's a perfect time to invite Grandma or an older neighbor. And of course, there's always room for your stuffed animals, who make charming guests on these occasions. They seem to enjoy dressing up as much as we do. Most stuffed animals are terribly polite at tea parties. They're good listeners and hardly ever say the wrong thing.

TEA'S ON

The ideal time for a tea party is four o'clock, but anytime between three and five will do. That's the traditional time for these get-togethers in England, where they originated.

How to brew the perfect pot

1 Heat a kettle of freshly drawn cold water on the stove.

2 Rinse out the tea pot with hot water.

3 Add one rounded teaspoon of loose tea to the infuser for each cup of tea, and include one extra "for the pot." Or, use one teabag for every two cups of tea with an extra bag for the pot.

4 When the water comes to a rolling boil, fill the teapot.

5 Let the tea steep for 3 to 5 minutes.

6 Serve in teacups with a tad of milk or lemon. Pour and enjoy!

Plain & *Fancy*

No tea party is complete without some sort of tasty treat. Cookies or tea biscuits are fine. But traditional tea time sandwiches are absolutely divine. Here are three common varieties:

1. Sliced egg and watercress
2. Sliced cucumber and dill
3. Salmon and cream cheese

And here are three more, not as traditional, but just as delicious:

4. Peanut butter and jelly (or honey)
5. Cream cheese and jelly (or cream cheese with olives)
6. Just jelly (marmalade is perfect!)

First, cut the crusts off the bread to make the sandwiches dainty. (The crusts can be used later for bread crumbs, bread pudding, or as a meal for wild birds.)

Don't overstuff the sandwiches. Tea-time fare is traditionally light, so it won't interfere with the evening meal.

Cut the sandwiches into triangles and arrange them artfully on the fanciest dish you have. If you prepare the sandwiches in advance, cover them and store them in the refrigerator.

Other traditional tea-time treats are scones (biscuits made from barley flour) and crumpets, which are muffins that have been fried in a pan.

There you have it! A perfect recipe for fun and make-believe.

A simple recipe for Lemon Scones

Preheat your oven to 450°F (230°C). Now get a medium-sized bowl, and mix together:

4	cups (1 L) whole wheat pastry flour
4	teaspoons (20 ml) baking powder
1 1/2	teaspoons (6 ml) baking soda
1	teaspoon (5 ml) salt

Stir in:

3 1/2	tablespoons (48 ml) lemon rind
2/3	cup (150 ml) margarine

Mix the whole thing together. It should resemble coarse meal.

Now mix these two together:

1 1/2	cups (375 ml) buttermilk
4	tablespoons (50 ml) honey

Pour this mixture into the center of your flour mixture and blend it. Knead the dough on a floured board until it's smooth (3 or 4 times). Roll the dough out, so it's about 1/2" (1 cm) thick. Cut the dough into 2" (5 cm) rounds (use the top of a small glass) and arrange the rounds on cookie sheets. Don't grease the cookie sheet. Brush the tops with half-and-half.

Bake the scones at 450°F (230°C) for 15 minutes, or until they're golden. Serve them immediately with butter, jam, or anything else you like. Hey, you did it yourself! Congratulations!

MUSIC! MUSIC! MUSIC!

The Magic of Music

THE MAGIC OF MUSIC

All right, kids from one to eighty — get ready to put out some sounds! Because music is for everyone! Whether you're by yourself or with a group, you can make music. Whether you sing like a nightingale or squawk like a crow, you can make music. Even if you can't carry a tune, you can still drum out a beat. That's music making, too!

Music expresses the feelings, the joys, and the passions inside each one of us. It can touch us, strengthen us, free us, and soothe us like nothing else can. No wonder the ancients called music a gift from the gods. And the gift is just waiting for you to come along and unwrap it.

Keep it simple

Learning just a few basics in music is all you really need to put out some incredible sounds.

Think about *a cappella* singing; that is, a voice without any instruments at all. Imagine that someone is on a beautiful walk in the country. Suddenly, he bursts out in song. That's just one voice plus one feeling, but it adds up to so much more — music magic at work.

Or how about this piece of musical magic: Just by memorizing both the words and the tune of a song you like, you give yourself the power to sing that song whenever you want, for yourself or others. The simple act of learning the words and melody has enhanced your musical powers incredibly!

The rule of simplicity applies to adding rhythm, too. Keeping the beat of a song simple and steady, even if it's done with only the clap of hands, will add tremendously to any musical experience.

Burn this secret in your mind for truly amazing results in music: Start simple, and stay simple, and you'll never go wrong.

An instrument that's easy to come by

Whether you realize it or not, you already own one of the finest musical instruments ever made. It's very small, but it can make a tremendous sound. It's versatile, too, making all sorts of tones, from coos to crowing. This instrument is extremely light and easy to carry, too. In fact, you carry it everyplace you go!

It's your voice box, of course — that little vibrating drum inside your throat. Usually, you use it for speech. But add the pixie dust of music and — tra-la, you'll get song!

What makes a good singer?

If you wonder whether you are a good singer, think about this: Your voice, and everyone else's, is as unique and distinct as a face, or a fingerprint! Part of the magic of singing is that everyone does it differently.

Now, it's true that some people are born with singing voices that others will line up to hear. Jazz musicians call these magical voices "pipes," or "chops."

You just might be one of these lucky people! After all, not every person with pipes is a professional singer. Many are ordinary folks with extraordinary voices. Their singing may or may not ever make them millions, but it certainly will provide them and those around them with a lot of pleasure, if they'll just open up and sing.

But what if you're pretty sure you don't have chops? Then think about this: Some of the world's most successful singers were born with ordinary voices at best. Artists like Mick Jagger, Rod Stewart, or the late Satchmo Armstrong succeeded because of their powerful ability to communicate — not because of their angelic singing voices.

So if the question is: Who can be a good singer? The answer is: Everybody!

Make the best of your voice

For most people, singing is just plain fun. It's a way to get your feelings out and to join with other people to make musical magic. Remember, even so-called ordinary singers can get better, too, with practice and a little technique.

Being relaxed, standing up straight and easy, and having well-exercised lungs all improve the sound of the human voice.

EXPLORING YOUR VOICE

Take a minute to explore your voice. Put your hand on your throat and hum. Feel the vibration inside your neck. Take a big breath and open your mouth to let out a vowel sound, like an ah or an oh. How low can you make the sound go? Explore the bottom of your voice. Try making different vowel sounds.

Now bring the tone up. Did the vibration in your throat move? Keep moving higher. How high can your voice go? Be careful not to shriek or strain your voice. (Even though you didn't pay a lot of money for it, the human voice is still a delicate instrument that deserves good care.)

How softly can you sing before your throat stops vibrating? How loud can you make your voice? Are you surprised by how much sound is inside you, just waiting to come out?

CALLING ALL VOICES

The pleasures of music-making shoot way up when you share the experience with a friend or two, or three, four or more! Why not corral some family or friends to join your musical explore? Most people, even shy ones, would love to have a chance to sing. And lots of people have songbooks and sheet music somewhere around the house that they can bring to a music session. So don't be shy. Put the call out that others are welcome!

MELODY MEDLEY

Here are three songs that you, or someone close to you, are sure to know.

1. *When the Saints Go Marching In*
2. *Swing Low, Sweet Chariot*
3. *Good Night, Ladies*

What's that you say? You know the tunes but you're not sure if you remember the words? Well, that's perfect! Because when you're performing a melody medley, you don't need words. In fact, words just confuse the matter. The magic of this musical medley is strictly in the tunes.

Here's how it's done:

Get three or more people together in a circle so that you can all see each other. One person will be the leader for each of the three songs. Start by humming "When the Saints Go Marching In," to make sure that everyone knows the melody. Clapping hands, or tapping out the beat, helps keep the song moving along, but don't let the tempo get ahead of you. Keep a good steady rhythm.

The person, or group, who hums "When the Saints Go Marching In," will stick to this melody throughout the entire medley. Their job is to stay with their song, no matter what. When it ends, they simply start it over.

And that's where the fun begins. Because after "Saints," comes melody number 2, "Swing Low, Sweet Chariot." At the end of "Swing Low," melody number 3 will be added on — "Good Night, Ladies."

Now, it may sound as if humming three songs at the same time will produce a dreadful mishmash of melodies. Well, you'll just have to try it yourself to find out. These three melodies, when combined without words, happen to come out as wonderful harmony.

Once you've got this set of songs down, you might try to see if there are other songs that can be added to the medley. Try "Amazing Grace," or "She'll Be Coming Round the Mountain," or "The Crawdad Song." The secret is in keeping the rhythm steady, and being prepared to hear new melodies without wavering from your own.

P. S. Melody medley works great with kazoos, too.

RAPPIN', RHYME, AND RHYTHM

In rap, the voice is used as a drum. Rap music is made from rhymed lyrics (words) spoken to a syncopated beat. (Syncopation is rhythm with the emphasis off the usual beat.) In rap, words are spoken off the beat, usually in rhymed couplets. The result is rap. The term rap, by the way, is a shortened form of the word *rapport*, because that is what rappers offer their audience.

Once you hear a rap song, you'll probably be inspired to concoct one of your own. Remember that in rap, the words act as a drum, keeping the syncopated, funky beat. This is rap:

Why don't you CHOOSE some WORDS,
Just like the ONES you HEARD . . .

This is not rap:

You've GOT to CHOOSE
The WORDS to USE . . .

Giving it away

No matter what kind of music you make, the best thing you can ever do with it is to give it away. Whether you have a rap group or a jug band, or just know a few songs to lead a sing-along, sharing your musical skills and talent gives people a lift that's really appreciated. Even sad songs seem to make people happier in the end!

So don't be shy. Share your music. Share it with your family and friends. Share it with little kids and the older people you know. Once you're ready, and it won't be long, call up a day-care center or a senior citizens' home, and ask if you, or you and your band, can come perform the music you know. Nine times out of ten, the answer will be an enthusiastic, "Yes!"

By sharing the gift of music, you'll be putting out good vibrations that will help the whole planet spin to a happier beat.

MARACAS

Maracas are Mexican rhythm makers, sometimes made by seeds shaken in a gourd. You can make some very fine maracas by filling empty plastic containers with a handful of rice or unpopped popcorn. Make at least two for each music maker so that each person can shake out the beat with two hands. Have fun painting these with wild designs and colors. (If the paint won't stick, add a little liquid soap to it.) The sound these instruments make is excellent!

PAPER BAG MARACAS

These simple instruments are fun and easy to make. Simply decorate a small paper bag, and place some rice or dry lentils in it. Then blow into the bag, tie with a rubber band, and shake, shake, shake!

CYMBALS

Two pot lids banged together make classic kitchen cymbals. Hold by the handles on top and strike lightly, loosely, and sparingly. This homemade instrument is loud and should only be used for musical emphasis! If you only have one lid, tap it with a rubber mallet, or wooden spoon — not metal — for the optimum sound.

TERRIFIC TAMBOURINES

For terrific tempo-keeping tambourines, punch holes around a couple of aluminum pie plates with a paper hole puncher. Then, use wire garbage bag ties to attach anything that jingles — jingle bells are great, but so are unused keys or buttons or paper clips. For dramatic effect when you're shaking the tambourine, string colorful ribbons through a few of the holes.

Would you believe that there's music even in something as humble as a rubber band? Well, there is! Kitchen glasses can be sparkling singers, too. Pots, pans, dishes, cans — all have music magic in them, when you know how to conjure it.

Homemade instruments are fun to make and fool around with. You can make a whole bandful of them in an afternoon, too — rhythm, string, and wind instruments. They're especially good to make with (and for) little kids who can usually come up with a few original ideas of their own.

HOMEMADE RHYTHM

Keeping the beat is the basis of music, more than almost anything else. When you've got a good beat, the music really keeps coming. It gets a life of its own, and takes on a flow. The right rhythm carries a music maker on.

Of course, you've already used a rhythm instrument every time you've clapped your hands or stamped your feet. And there are many other rhythm instruments that are yours just for the making.

WATER MUSIC

Drinking glass chimes

A lovely sparkling sound can be made with simple kitchen glasses filled with water and tapped with a spoon. You make different notes by filling the glasses with different amounts of water. The more water, the higher the tone. A drop of food coloring in the glasses adds to the charm and makes it easier to remember which note is which.

For the sake of simplicity, start with three notes. Fill your glasses to three different levels for three notes of the scale, going up one after another — as in "do, re, mi." (If you prefer numbers, it's 1, 2, 3.) For now, let's call the notes Low, Middle, High, and write them L, M, H.

Here are three songs to perform on your 3-note set of drinking glass chimes. Each letter represents one tap on the glass. Relax your hand and hold the spoon as lightly as possible and you'll get a fuller, richer tone.

HOT CROSS BUNS

Hot Cross Buns
H   M   L
Hot Cross Buns
H   M   L
One a penny
L   LL   L
Two a penny
M   MM   M
Hot Cross Buns
H   M   L

Merrily We Roll Along

Merrily we roll along
H M L M H H H
Roll along
M   MM
Roll along
H   H H
Merrily we roll along
H M L M H H H
O'er the deep blue sea.
M   M   H   M   L

A french folk song

Try this pattern on your glasses in a steady beat that is not too fast, and it will probably sound familiar to you.

L L L M <u>H M</u> L H M M <u>L</u>
(then, repeat)

Note: The underlined notes should be held for two beats each. That means you wait a beat before going on to the next note.

GLASS CHIME ROUNDS

A round is a song that harmonizes with itself. Thus, if the song is started by one singer, then added to by another during the first measures into the melody, the result is harmony, not chaos.

"Row, Row, Row Your Boat" is a round that most people know. It's fun to sing, and it also makes a charming song when played on drinking glass chimes.

Here's how to do it:

Prepare six glasses at six different levels of water for six notes: do, re, mi, fa, so, and a higher octave do. (If you prefer identifying notes by numbers, prepare 1, 2, 3, 4, 5, and 8.)

Let each music maker stand on the opposite side of the set of glasses, if possible, at least until the song is mastered. If you've got more than one set of glasses filled, of course, that's even better. Then each music maker can have his own.

Row Row Row Your Boat Gently Down The Stream

1   1 1   2   3   3 2 3   4 5

Merrily Merrily Merrily Merrily Life Is But A Dream

8 8 8 5 5 5 3 3 3 1 1 1   5   4 3 2 1

HOMEMADE STRINGS

One of the best sounding homemade instruments can be made with just an empty tissue box and a few rubber bands! So-called designer tissue boxes, ones that have the opening on two sides, work especially well, but any kind will do just fine.

Here's what to do:

Rustle up a variety of rubber bands — thin ones, wide ones, and everything in between. Put a few around the box, where the cut out part is. Experiment to find out which rubber bands make the best sounds. Play this instrument by plucking it, and you will be surprised what a good tone it makes. That is because the tissue container functions as a sound box, amplifying and enriching the sound.

Two-by-four guitar

This creation also uses rubber bands to create stringed sounds.

Get a plain wooden board, 2" x 4" (5 cm x 10 cm) or 1" x 4" (2.5 cm x 10 cm) (it doesn't matter). In fact, any narrow piece of wood will do. Hammer in three or four nails at either end. Add a *bridge* by nailing a cross piece of wood. (You can use an empty tissue box as a bridge, too, adding to the basic design given above.)

Now attach rubber bands to each set of nails, and pull them fairly tight. (The thinner and tighter you stretch them, the higher the note they make.)

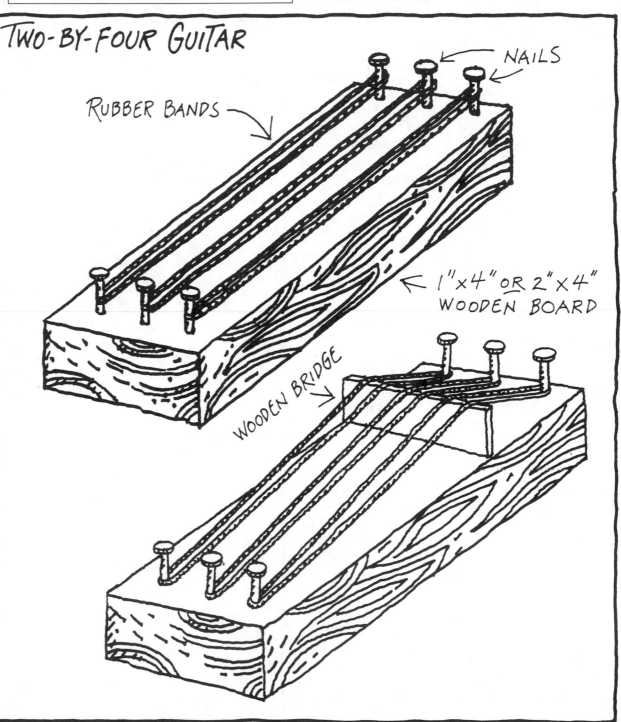

TWO-BY-FOUR GUITAR

NAILS

RUBBER BANDS

1" x 4" OR 2" x 4" WOODEN BOARD

WOODEN BRIDGE

Make a boom-bah

What's that? You've never heard of a boom-bah? Then you've never made a visit to the Leather Corner Post Hotel and Restaurant in Fogelsville, PA. That's the Home of the Boom-bahs, where you can hear booming and bahhing every Friday night. But don't worry. You don't have to travel to Fogelsville to find one of these unique and fascinating instruments. You can make one of your very own! That's what folks in Fogelsville do, and they are experts on boom-bahs.

Boom-bahs are a little like snowflakes — each one is a unique creation, never to be duplicated. An old pogo stick is the ideal spine for this unique instrument, but a broom stick with a rubber foot on the end does nicely, too. Pie plates, bottle caps, keys, jingle bells, and baby rattles, all make good additions.

Here is a picture of a sample boom-bah. But remember, everyone has to create their own design for this unique instrument.

Playing the boom-bah

You can use your boom-bah as a One-Man Band instrument, singing along while you beat out the rhythm by stomping the boom-bah on the floor. But in the case of the boom-bah, more are better. A bunch of boom-bahs stomping together really make for lots of fun.

At the Leather Corner Post Hotel and Restaurant, boom-bahhers stomp along to songs on the juke boxes, to every conceivable style of song, from polka to disco. You and your boom-bah group can do the same, to records or the radio.

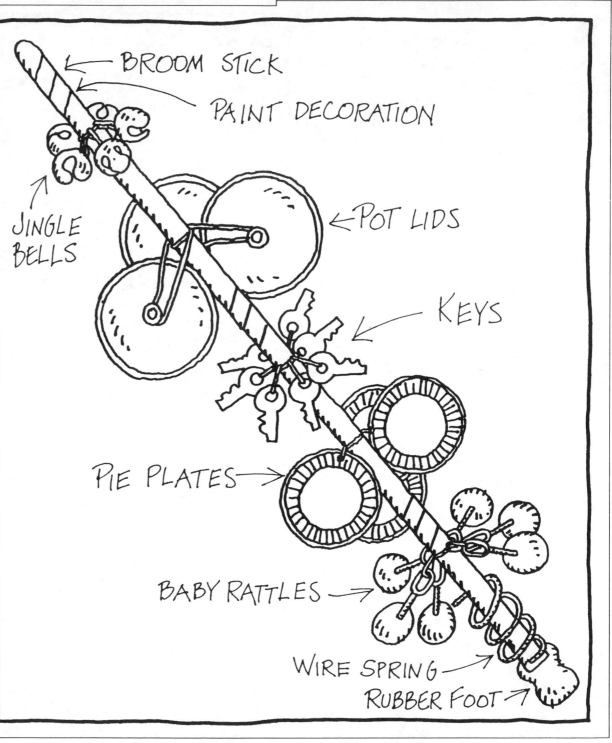

STRIKE UP THE BAND

If you like getting together with a bunch of people to make music, and you'd like to do more of it, think about forming a band or chorus. It's amazing how much you can grow when you join with others and spend a little time practicing and rehearsing music. Even if you never perform in public, you'll have loads of fun as your musical skills multiply.

You can form a short-term band that rehearses for a day and gives a performance at night. Or, your band can become an on-going concern, rehearsing most weekends and performing around town as opportunities arise.

The same group of people can even do both, changing their band's identity to suit their needs for each performance.

Don't forget a name for your band. Try to make the name express who you are, and what kind of music you like to play and sing. For instance:

MAMA AND THE BLUES FAMILY

THE JAZZY JONES'S

THE ROCKIN' ROBINSONS

THE COUNTRY COUSINS

THE MAIN STREET MUSIC MACHINE

A Jug Band

An old-fashioned jug band is fun to put together, and fairly simple, too. Music like the melody medley and blues (when played to a lively beat) fits right into a jug band format. So do all sorts of folk songs and any other kind of down home, old-fashioned, easy-playing mountain music.

Instruments that really add pizzaz to a jug band are guitars, fiddles, harmonicas, all and any homemade instruments, and of course, a jug to blow into. (A vegetable grater makes a good substitute for a washboard, if you don't have one.)

With only a little time and commitment, your jug band will be able to put on quite a show. Go on a scavenger hunt to find straw hats, checkered shirts, overalls, flowery dresses, and army boots to wear as costumes when your jug band gives a concert. Anyone who's not singing can chew on a corn cob pipe, stamp his feet, and let loose with an occasional "yee haw" to liven up the already lively show.

BACKYARD FUN
Bug Hunt

What are bugs really?

They creep. They crawl. They swim. They twirl, leap, and fly. They can walk upside down on the ceiling. Some even glow in the dark! Bugs are amazing creatures! And considering that there are about four million of them for every acre on earth, you'd think we humans would know a lot about them.

Simply put, bugs are small animals — the most numerous on planet earth. They're also the oldest. Some were here before the dinosaurs! Think of it — the great Tyrannosaurus Rex and Stegosaurus roamed the earth, squishing the ancestors of the very beetles and ants that live in your backyard today.

Since they've been around so long, insects have learned to adapt to all sorts of conditions, from ice ages to earthquakes, from famines to wars. They are nature's all time, number one, ablest survivors. No wonder we have so much to learn from them. And you can begin exploring right in your own backyard.

BUG-HUNTING

When you go on a bug hunt, you'll discover a new and fascinating world, right beneath your feet. This world is populated with creatures who look like they're straight out of science fiction. But there's no make believe here. The strange miniature beings you'll discover will be real and alive!

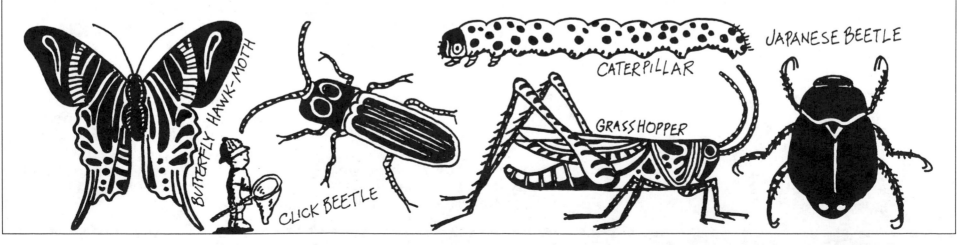

BUTTERFLY HAWK-MOTH

CLICK BEETLE

CATERPILLAR

GRASSHOPPER

JAPANESE BEETLE

What you'll need for bug hunting:

A keen eye (Like all wildlife, bugs are masters of camouflage.)

Clean, clear containers with air holes or netting on top

Trowel, or large spoon to collect specimens

Notebook to write down and sketch the insects you find

An overripe banana and a spoonful of brown sugar

Magnifying glass (optional)

Microscope (optional)

For nighttime bug-hunting:

All of the above, plus a flashlight.

Be prepared!

As with every adventure, you face risks on a bug hunt. Even though the vast majority of insects are perfectly harmless, there are a few aggressors who will be out there hunting you! You are already familiar with these pests — like certain flies and mosquitoes.

Different people have different bug-warding-off techniques. Some say eating garlic makes a human less palatable to mosquitoes. Others exclaim about the wonders of peppermint oil, rubbed on ankles, neck, and ears. Experiment with other scents. Something will work for you if you keep trying.

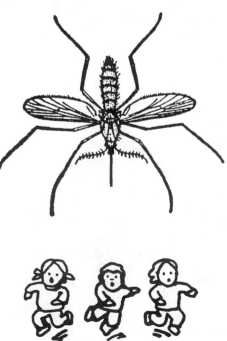

THE SCIENTIFIC APPROACH

The word *insect* is a scientific term. An insect is an air-breathing creature with six legs, no backbone, and a body made up of three main parts — head, thorax (chest), and abdomen.

The word "bug" is sometimes a scientific term, too. There's a family of insects called *bugs*, or *true bugs*. They also breathe air, have six legs, and three body parts. True bugs always have a triangle on their thorax, in back of their heads. That's the way scientists identify them.

Unofficially, a bug can be any insect or other creepy crawler that we find in the garden, grass, or woods. Centipedes, pill bugs, and spider mites are examples of creatures that look a lot like insects or true bugs, but, scientifically speaking, really aren't.

Insect or bug

Is it an insect, true bug, or another kind of creepy crawler? That's one of the first questions to ask about the creatures you'll find on your bug hunt.

If it's an insect, you'll be able to see its three main body parts — head, thorax, and abdomen. The head will have feelers or antennae. These may be like sticks or like feathers. The insect's legs and wings are always attached to the thorax.

If you know it's an insect, but don't know it's name, ask yourself which major group it seems to fit in. Is it a beetle? Fly? Caterpillar? You can give the creature a descriptive name of your own choosing until you learn if it has one. But since there are many undiscovered species in the world, you just may discover one of your own!

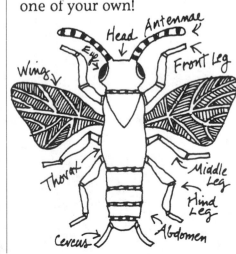

SPECIAL MESSAGE TO BUG HATERS

First of all, if bugs give you the creeps, you're not alone. Many people fear and dislike these strange little creatures. Some kill them on sight! Others shriek and run away whenever they spot one.

If you are one of these people, think about this: Bugs and insects are an important part of our world. Even though some need to be controlled at times, they are great assistants to Mother Nature. Just by doing what comes naturally, they help keep our soil healthy. Healthy soil means healthy crops and gardens for people!

Insects are also a great source of nutrition for birds. So if you like birds, be thankful for bugs! Giving a bug a funny name can help you:

1. Get over your fear

2. Remember it more clearly

3. Try harder to protect it

Scientific (Latin) names for bugs:

Lepidoptera = *Butterflies and Moths*

Orthoptera = *Grasshoppers, Crickets, Katydids, Cockroaches, etc.*

Coleoptera = *Beetles*

Isoptera = *Termites*

Homoptera = *Aphids*

Diptera = *Flies*

Hymenoptera = *Bees, Wasps, Ants, etc.*

Phantom-of-the-optera = *The most horrible bugs imaginable!*

Hello, Gorgeous

Do bugs make you shudder because they're so ugly or weird looking? Then remember, looks aren't everything. If you saw the movie *E.T.*, you'll remember the wrinkled little space alien who won the hearts of those around him. Why not think of the bugs you meet as friendly aliens?

Where to look

Many bugs are green, black, or brown. They blend in with the natural scene so that their enemies cannot easily spot them. This is called camouflage. But if you know where to look, you will surely find success on your hunt.

Check the ground and the base of trees and bushes for insects. Peek deep inside any flowers that are in bloom and check under leaves growing on the stems of plants. Turn over a rock to find crawling creatures. Look under loose bark for caterpillars.

Sugaring

One sure-fire way to attract bugs is to put out some sweet smelling food for them to eat. All you need for this is an over-ripe banana and some brown sugar. Mix these together and let them sit for a couple of hours. Then, go out and paint the gooey substance on the bark of a tree. Now all you have to do is wait. One by one, insects will soon appear, attracted by the scent of the sweet stuff you've lured them with.

You can sugar after dark, too. Put the substance out before dusk, and return with a flashlight after nightfall. Are there more bugs at the sugar now than in the day? Count the different kinds of insects you've attracted. Are there more than you imagined, or fewer? What kinds of animals appeared at the sugar? Observe them as they eat. Are there any beetles on the tree? How about caterpillars, moths, or ants?

While you're out "hunting," why not keep a record? Bring some drawing paper and colored pens, pencils, or crayons, and make some sketches. Write down the date and time you saw the creature, and how many of them you saw.

LIVE AND LET LIVE

You don't have to kill or hurt a bug to study it. If you wish to observe the insects you find, simply "borrow" them from the wild for a short time by placing them in clean, clear containers. Prepare the containers by adding a little dirt and leaf mold (dead leaves), as well as a bottle-cap full of water. A few sticks with green leaves add a nice touch, too, to make your bug feel at home. Cover the top with a piece of net, or waxed paper, into which tiny holes have been pricked with a straight pin.

If you want to borrow a caterpillar or other creature from Mother Nature for a while, be sure to include, in its guest quarters, fresh, green leaves of whatever plant you found it on. Most likely, if you found the crawler on a particular plant, that plant is the animal's major food source. Don't borrow a creature for too long, though. Bugs have short lives and plenty of important environmental work to do. Return your bug to the exact place you found him after no more than twenty-four hours.

But if you find a dead bug, use it

You'll probably come across some creature corpses from time to time, though. Look for them inside window- sills, and under bushes. They can be kept separately, and studied by you, or used as lures to study ants. You may also find some empty insect skins! Yes, many insects shed their external skeletons as they grow too big for them. These shed skeleton-skins make great souvenirs.

SUPER STARS AND CIRCUS PERFORMERS

Some bugs and insects have special talents that put them in a class all their own. Look for these talented tricksters on your bug hunt.

Special effects — the firefly

For dazzling special effects, the firefly tops the list. This amazing creature literally lights up the summer sky with her pyrotechnics!

Technically, she's a beetle, not a fly. If you meet her by day, she appears to be an ordinary striped creature with not much in the way of special talents. But at night, she steals the show as she flashes out pulsing light, sending off signals to attract a mate.

The singing weathermen — a cricket chorus

If you live near grass and trees, chances are you've heard many free concerts performed by a chorus of chirping crickets. The chorus performs nightly in summer, changing its tempo to match the temperature. The hotter the weather, the faster it sings.

Amazingly, you can calculate the temperature in Fahrenheit degrees by counting the chirps crickets make in 14 seconds, and then adding 42. The result is incredibly accurate!

A circus clown — introducing the click beetle

If you come across a click beetle in your backyard, you're in for a treat. These clownish creatures, with two false eyes on their backs, have a circus-style trick they can perform, with a little help from a friend like you.

Gently pick up the beetle, who is a perfectly nice creature who will not hurt you in any way. Then, lay it down again, on its back, and step back to give him room to do his trick. The beetle will slowly bend in the middle. Then — pow! It will pop straight up into the air, letting out a loud "click" as it does. Like a true professional, the click beetle will land on its feet, ready for applause.

Military might — the bombardier beetle

You may have a piece of living field artillery walking around in your backyard. It's a small, tan and orange beetle with pretty, blue-black wings. Don't let these delicate looks deceive you. This beetle is armed and dangerous! It's got a fully functioning, retractible cannon in its rear end, and it will use it if it has to!

If an enemy approaches, such as a small twig held by you which gently taps the creature, the bombardier beetle will rear up and fire off his bomb of caustic chemicals, with a pop and a puff of blue smoke! Look, but don't touch! The bomb can actually burn your hand!

Lucky charms — house crickets

Some crickets, called house crickets, or hearth crickets, seem to prefer living indoors to out. Throughout the ages, people have said that meeting up with such a cricket will bring on a spell of good luck.

Do you have a house or hearth cricket living in your house or backyard? If you find one, test out the ancient belief about their bringing good luck. Watch for lucky occurrences in the week after you come across the cricket. You never know. . . .

ANT OBSERVATIONS

One group of animals that you will surely find on your bug hunt is ants. These legendary workers are always busy in any backyard, in the city as well as the country. Often you will find them marching in a trail as they go about their business of helping the whole colony to survive.

Unlike many other insects, ants are social creatures, who live in a large nest with hundreds of their fellows. In fact, a single ant could not survive on its own. The fate of every single ant is tied up to the fate of his entire nest.

Mark an individual and get on his case

Since ants tend to look alike to us, it's a good idea to mark an ant or two when you are observing them. A teeny dab (far less than a drop) of bright quick drying paint will not hurt their hard shells at all. Apply it gently with the narrow end of a toothpick. Then, watch how your marked ant interacts with the rest of his group.

Mark the first ant who finds the food at your sugar lure. What does he do? Does he stay and eat? Does he alert others in the nest?

You can challenge the ants you're observing, too. It's interesting to give them a problem and see how they'll handle it, too. If you have a dead fly, pin it to the ground not far from the ant nest with a long needle or straight pin. Mark the first ants who come along and find it. They will try to move the fly. Do they seem baffled when it does not budge? What will they do? How will they solve the problem?

Okay, Bug-hunters — are you ready to go off on your explore? Got your notebook? Got a pencil? Got your curiosity ready? Don't forget your sugar and a little patience.

Because millions and millions of bugs are out there now, waiting for you. Just like they have been since the dawn of time.

BACKYARD CAMPING

THE CALL OF THE WILD IN YOUR OWN BACKYARD

If you long to sleep out under the starry sky, there's no better place to start than right at home. Yes, your own backyard is the perfect place to have an outdoor adventure. It's fun for the whole family or something exciting to do with a friend.

Tenting

If you already have a tent or can borrow or buy one, great. A small pup tent can easily accommodate two kids. If the whole family or neighborhood friends are joining in the camp-out, keep in mind that two small tents might be a better choice than one big one.

If you don't have a tent to use, don't be discouraged; you'll still be able to camp out. With a little help from some blankets and perhaps a tablecloth, you'll be able to rig up a very service-able shelter. The same is true if you don't have a sleeping bag. In fact, one of the great things about backyard camping is that you don't need much of anything — except a spooky story or two.

To make a sleeping bag that will stay together all night, try folding and pinning a blanket like this:

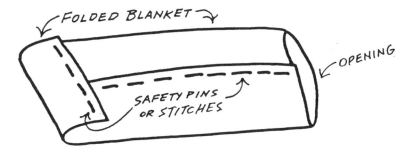

Use giant-sized safety pins, enough to do the job well, and be sure they are facing toward the outside of the blanket. If you don't have any pins, you can baste the blanket with strong thread or even dental floss. The stitches can be as much as 6" (15 cm) apart, as long as the thread is strong. Basting the blanket should take less than twenty minutes.

WHAT TO BRING

True, in backyard camping you don't have to trek up a mountain with a heavy backpack full of gear, but you still need to have certain things on hand. Depending on how roughly you want to rough it, pack sparsely and efficiently. (No fair going "home" to get things you forgot!)

Water can be carried in a couple of half-gallon containers. Food can be packed in an insulated picnic case. Individual boxes of cereal come in handy for snacking and breakfast.

Flashlights with fresh batteries, one for each camper, are a must, and so are a few candles and matches. Make sure the candles are the fat kind that are less likely to fall over. Anchor them firmly in a sturdy candle holder, keep them away from blankets, and blow them out before going to sleep.

Some campers bring playing cards or harmonicas on their outings, too. The harmonica is one of the most versatile intruments around, and it's fun for making up music on.

USE CLEAN PLASTIC SODA BOTTLES FOR WATER

FLASHLIGHT

EXTRA BATTERIES

PICNIC CASE WITH CEREAL & SNACKS

TENT SHOULD FACE SOUTHEAST

JOES CAMP

BANDANA

SWEATER   SOCKS

HOME SWEET CAMPSITE

Choosing the right location for your backyard campsite won't be difficult, but keep a few things in mind. Your tent should be pitched on flat ground if possible. Also, if it faces southeast, you'll wake up to the first rays of sunrise and the warmth that sunshine brings.

You can personalize your campsite by giving it a name or hanging out a flag or pennant. A flag can be made from any piece of strong rectangular cloth, tied or tacked to a pole outside the tent. A sign can be made on sturdy cardboard and leaned up against the nearest tree.

What to wear

When camping, comfort comes first. Be sure your clothes are roomy. Even if you're camping out in summer, pack a sweater and extra socks. The night air can be surprisingly chilly.

One item every camper should have is a bandana. This one small piece of material has a lot of uses at a campsite. It can cool you when it's hot or cover your head if it rains. It also makes a good carrying case, especially when it's tied to the end of a stick. At night, if you suspect there are raccoons around, you can use it to hang your breakfast food from the branch of a tree.

KNOTS

What's that you say? You don't how to tie a clove hitch knot? How about a square knot? Knot tying is so useful when camping (and at other times, too) that this may be the perfect time to learn.

Now, it's one thing to look at a picture of squiggly lines on a page, and it's another to learn to tie knots. If you are serious about mastering a couple of knots, you are going to need two things. The first is a rope or a length of strong twine to practice on. The second thing is patience. Lots of it. Learning knots can be frustrating.

When to use a clove hitch
In a cowboy movie, when the hero ties up his horse so he can go propose to the school marm or go talk to the sheriff, he's usually tying the reins with a clove hitch knot. This knot is used for tying tent pegs and attaching guy lines. You can attach ropes to trees with it, and use it in the garden, too.

The square knot
Here's another useful camping knot that campers often use to tie up their gear.

COME AND GET IT!

Setting up a camp can make a camper hungry! And since eating out under the open sky is one of the biggest pleasures of camping, you'll want to be prepared to fix up some tasty dishes on your night out.

For backyard camping, you can cook inside or out. If you opt for the latter, use a barbecue or hibachi grill as your campfire.

Camping cuisine classics

 THE MENU

Hot dogs, C-Rations, baked beans, and S'Mores

HOT DOGS (and their vegetarian counterpart, Not Dogs, or Tofu Pups) are simple to prepare, and delicious. Just slit the dog and cook it till it's plump and juicy. Pop it into a roll toasted on the grill, serve with relish, mustard or even sauerkraut, and yum . . . .

C-RATIONS are any uncooked food that begins with the letter, C. Cut-up carrots, cucumbers, cauliflower, celery, and chips are good to start with; crackers and cheese add to the menu, too.

BAKED BEANS are an American camping classic if there ever was one. Buy them in cans and cook in a small pot until they're good and hot. Baked beans have long been a favorite of cowboys and other campers. They make good leftovers later on, too, when there's no refrigerator to raid.

S'MORES are the classic camping treat. Their strange name comes from words people say as soon as they taste them — "some more"! Of course, with a full mouth of delicious goo, the words don't come out so clearly. Hence, "S'mores"!

Have on hand marshmallows, a box of graham crackers and some flat chocolate bars. Put a marshmallow over the fire until it cooks. Have two crackers and some chocolate ready. When the marshmallow is good and gooey, slip it onto the chocolate and place it in between the graham crackers like a sandwich. The hot marsh-mallows will melt the chocolate and warm the crackers. Pop a bite of this gooey deliciousness in your mouth and you'll definitely want S'more!

Dictionary

A great daytime game for campers. You'll need a dictionary, and several pencils and pieces of paper. Hand one of each out to all the players. Then, one person looks up a word in the dictionary — a word he or she thinks no one will know the meaning of! That person reads the word out loud, and the others have to write down a definition. If nobody guesses, the person who found the word gets a point. If somebody does get the right answer, that person is the one who gets the point. Players take turns selecting words. Most points wins. The fun, of course, is in how wrong some guesses can be, and what funny definitions people can make up, when they know they don't know the answer!

Reveille and Taps

Reveille (re-vuh-lee) and Taps are the trumpet fanfares that announce wake-up time and bedtime. In case you didn't know it, there are words to Taps, and they make a great finale for your evening camp-out. The words are best sung quietly and thoughtfully, and as slowly as possible:

Day is done;
Gone the sun
From the hill,
From the lake,
From the sky...
All is well;
Safely rest...
God is nigh.

AFTER NIGHTFALL

When the sun goes down, the music or star-gazing can begin. Now is the time to bring out the guitar or reach for a harmonica. If you've got someone who can play three chords on the guitar, you've got a choice of thousands of songs to sing.

Ghost stories are great around the campfire, too. Sit in a circle, so nobody can sneak up from behind! Now, take turns telling the spookiest story you can. Flashlights shone upward under the storytellers' chins are a must!

If you've been learning how to find the major constellations (see Star section, page 84), it's a good time to share your knowledge with a friend. Everybody likes to wish on stars, too, from tiny toddlers to senior citizens.

Okay, partners. You're as ready as you're going to be. So open up the back door, get a breath of the great outdoors, and head off into the wilds of your own backyard. Happy camping!

HOT WEATHER FUN

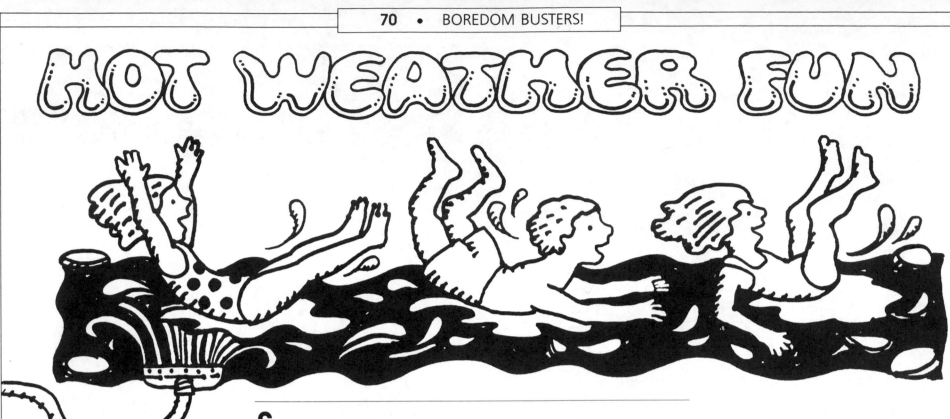

Some summer weekends, it's just too hot to do most things. So what do you do? Turn on the A/C and flop down in front of the boob tube? You could . . . or you could go outside and —

Make a water slide

You'll need a large plastic sheet, at least ten feet long, and a nice soft piece of grass to put it down on. You'll also want to have a good long space for a runway, to get up your speed before you take off! You'll also need a hose with a sprinkler.

You can pick up a plastic tarp at your local hardware store, if you haven't got anything that'll do. A 15' (5 m) one won't run you more than a dollar or so. These tarps aren't made to last, though. You might get an hour's worth of fun out of one before it rips to shreds. As an alternative, you can also buy thicker plastic sheeting that comes off a roll. It's more expensive, but will last for much longer — more than one summer, in fact.

When you've got your tarp ready, spread it out in a flat part of your lawn. You'll need to hold down the four corners somehow. Smooth-edged rocks are good — they won't scratch you if you bump into them. Large, plastic bowls filled with water will do a good job, too.

Now set up your sprinkler so that it "rains" on the tarp, making it good and slick. After a minute or two, try out your slide and see if it's good or if it needs adjusting.

To use the slide, take a running start, then slide down on your stomach, your back, or even on your feet! If you want to run down your slide, try making boots for yourself out of plastic bags, holding them on with rubber bands. These will help you slide better. Talk about wet and wild!

BLOW BUBBLES!

On hot, humid days, bubbles last longer, so now's the perfect time to blow some whoppers! And you don't even need to buy any from the store — you can make your own.

Start with liquid dishwashing soap. Mix it with an equal amount of water, and if you've got glycerine around the house, add an equal amount of that, too — it isn't necessary, but it sure helps make better bubbles. (You can get a bottle of glycerine at any pharmacy.) When you've put your ingredients together, shake them up well.

Now you need something to make your bubbles with. Some good "bubble machines" are:

The *rim of a plastic carton*. Use a clothespin for a handle. *Wire hanger*. You can twist them into a variety of shapes. Cut out the bottom of a *juice can* — the small kind that comes in six-packs. By blowing into the hole at the top, you've made a bubble pipe!

You can make a bubble frame out of *two straws and a string*. Just run the string through one straw, then back through the other, and tie a knot in it. The string should be long enough so that the final frame is in the shape of a square. Now, if you lower the whole frame into the bubble soap, holding the straws, then lift it out and snap the straws apart, you'll be making some mighty fine bubbles.

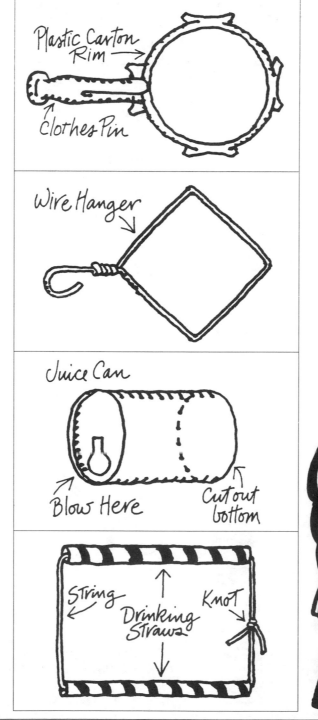

MAKE A SUN HAT

You don't want to get too much sun on a hot summer day, especially if you're fair-skinned. The top of your head is particularly sensitive. In order to keep from frying your brains, you might consider making one of a number of sun hats for yourself. Here are two simple kinds to make:

Folded paper hat

Start with a sheet of newspaper (two pages with a fold down the middle). Fold the outer edges down so they make a point at the top center. Fold the bottom flap up to meet the edge of the triangle. Fold it over again, and do the same on the other side. Roll up the front brim, and you've got yourself an instant hat!

Stitched hat

This comes from China originally, and was once called a Coolie Hat. You'll need:

Cardboard	
String or yarn	A large nail
A needle	A ruler
Heavy duty scissors	A pencil

Cut five cardboard triangles, about 10" (25 cm) on the sides, and about 6" (15 cm) at the base. Punch holes along the sides with your nail, about 1/4" (5 mm) from the edge and 1/2" (1 cm) apart. Lace the triangles together with your string. Punch two holes in the sides and tie on a pair of chin strings. Paint your hat if you want to, or use different colored cardboard.

MAKE YOUR OWN ICE CREAM

Ice cream has been around for thousands of years. You can buy it in any store. You can buy a fancy ice cream maker and make your own. OR — you can try the following recipe that's easy enough for any kid to follow!

Put these things in a pot:

1	cup (250 ml) of milk
1/2	cup (125 ml) of sugar
1/4	teaspoon (1 ml) of salt
3	beaten egg yolks

Cook the mixture gently, and don't stop stirring until it begins to bubble. Then put it in the freezer until it turns to slush.

MEANWHILE . . .

Get a mixing bowl. Put a cup of whipping cream in it, along with a teaspoon of vanilla. Beat it with an egg beater until the cream is whipped, and standing in soft peaks. Stop whipping now, or you'll ruin your ice cream. Pour your cold slush into the cream and mix it around, preferably without smashing your cream too much. Then freeze the mixture in ice trays or shallow pans till it's firm. It's best if you stir it a couple of times in the first hour. It should be ready to eat in three or four hours.

If vanilla's not your favorite, you can add chocolate syrup or fruit jam or nuts or chocolate chips or cinnamon. Add these things during the middle of the freezing process.

If the above recipe is too much for you to do, or you don't happen to have the ingredients, try making your own ices! It's even easier!

Get an ice cube tray and a box of toothpicks. Fill the trays with your favorite fruit juice. Put a toothpick in each square and freeze. Instant ices!

Frozen bananas

Cut some bananas in half and stick wooden skewers or Popsicle sticks in them. Freeze them. When they're frozen, take them out and dip them in melted chocolate. (You can melt chocolate bars or chocolate chips in the microwave or in the top of a double boiler.) You can also roll the bananas in nuts, granola, or gorp. Then re-freeze them, covered in aluminum foil. Wait till you taste them!

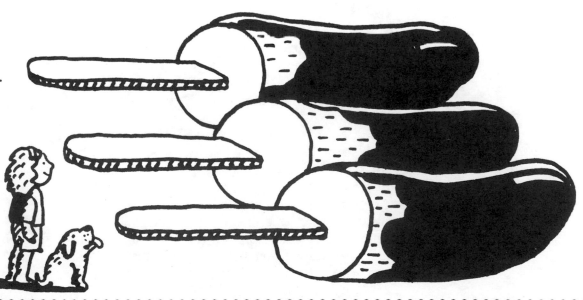

NATIVE AMERICAN FUN!

The life-style of many American Indian nations is one we can all learn from. Before colonists came to America's shores from other parts of the world, the very first Americans lived on the same land we live on now. And they lived in perfect harmony with nature. They knew the secrets of every rock, field, and stream. They knew how to care for the Earth and draw on and use her treasures without using them up!

Making a tepee

While some Native Americans lived in tepees, longhouses, and earth lodges, today many live in regular houses and apartments in cities and on reservations. You can learn about the tepees built by the Plains Indians by making your own.

To construct your own tepee you will need a little help from your local carpet store. Call to ask whether the store is willing to donate a few cardboard tubes that carpets and rugs are rolled in. Most stores are happy to provide you with them.

Gather 5 tubes and tie them together about 12" (30 cm) down from the top with a rope. (Here's another good time to use the clove hitch knot, page 68.) Stand all the tubes together in an upright position and then begin pulling them out, one by one, and little by little, to make a circle of space.

This will be the frame of your tepee. When you have a large enough space, cover the tepee with one or more blankets. Tuck them under the rope on top and fan them along the carpet rolls.

SEVENTH GENERATION

One of the most important ideas that Native Americans hold is that we "borrow the Earth from our children." Whenever they had to make a decision about how to use the land they lived on, they would ask, "how will this affect the children of the coming seven generations?" Migrating peoples made it their goal not to harm the Earth in any way. Whenever they left a campsite, they took great care to make sure it was left as pristine and natural a setting as they had found it. They were careful not to leave any evidence that they had even camped there!

You can share in the rich heritage of Native Americans. The ancestors of those who lived hundreds of years ago are eager for young people to learn about Native American ways.

Laughing Bird? Runs Like Deer?

Some Native Americans gave themselves new names every few years, or whenever a significant event happened in a member's life. The new name would reflect the growth that an individual had made over time.

American Indian names tell something about each individual's personality. Often, people were named after animals that they reminded others of.

If you were an American Indian, what name would suit you best?

INDIAN DRESS

Native Americans spoke several different languages, so when they came together — during powwows and bison hunts, for example — they used special symbols and sign language to understand one another. Some symbols and signs were used by all of the North American nations, but variations were common.

You can learn some Native American symbols by making a symbol collage. Try some of the examples shown here, or ask your local librarian for help finding a book on symbols.

The sign language many of the North American nations used was known as the Esperanto of the Plains Indians. Try a few of these signs on your own.

Friendship: Lift your right hand to the same level as your neck. Make sure your index and middle fingers are touching and the rest of your fingers are closed together. Then, raise your hand until it is even with your face.

Thank you: Open your hands, with the palms down, and extend them in front of you. Then, lower your hands as far as you can.

Color: Use the fingertips of your right hand to make a circle on the back of your left hand. Then, point to an object of the color you want to represent, like the sky for blue.

Earth: Extend both hands at chest-level, keeping them 7 inches (15 cm) apart. Then, slowly lower both hands until they're level with your thighs.

Totem pole

The Northwest Coast Indians, such as the Nishga and Tlinget, make tall totem poles that tell the history of their families much like a family tree does. They carve large tree trunks with the faces of special birds and animals to tell about their ancestors, as well as any special family history.

You can make a totem pole with several empty coffee cans. Add pebbles or sand to the cans to give them weight, then tape the covered cans together and cover them with butcher paper (newspaper will work, too). Add features such as eyes, ears, and mouths to each can.

Another way to make the pole is to give each friend a can to cover by gluing or taping construction paper to it. Then each individual can is decorated with colorful designs of faces and features from birds, animals, or your imagination.

When each can is decorated, add sand or pebbles for weight and tape them together.

Either of these ways will produce a totem pole you will be proud to display.

EMPTY COFFEE CAN →

BUTCHER PAPER
OR NEWSPAPER →

The council ring

In some American Indian groups, decisions were made around a council ring. The ring was the place where people came together to make plans and work out differences. Stories were often told to demonstrate proper behavior for members. In summer, council meetings were outdoors; in winter, they were in a tepee around a *council fire*.

The ideal setting for a council ring is under a grove of trees. To make a council ring, mark out a circle that is big enough to accommodate your friends and perhaps a couple of visitors. A circle of stones works well to mark out the ring, as do some well-placed sticks.

The council ring is the perfect place to hold a family meeting or to work out plans, or even problems, with others at the camp. Each person is given a chance to express himself or herself fully. But while it is permissible to argue within the council ring, the spirit of the ring is always one of mutual respect.

After everyone has spoken, the leader, usually the eldest person, calls for a period of quiet contemplation. Then, solutions and suggestions are called for. When everyone has given his full input, the leader sums up and, if necessary, gives a directive that is in the interest of the harmony of the group.

Much of the government we see in the United States and on reservations today is based on American Indian ideas. For example, the Iroquois Indians created their own constitution long before Thomas Jefferson was around, and Benjamin Franklin liked some of their ideas so much that he adopted them for the U.S. government.

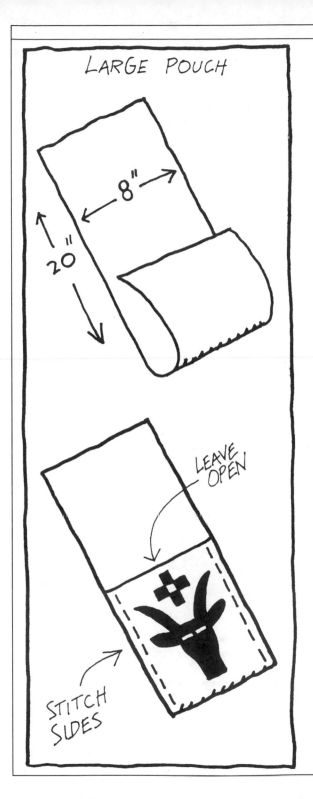

LARGE POUCH

8"

20"

LEAVE OPEN

STITCH SIDES

Lakota-Sioux pouch

The Lakota-Sioux Indians hunted animals like buffalo, moose, and rabbits for food and skins. The skins were then softened and used to make pouches. Medicine men, or healers, sometimes placed special herbs and charms in their pouches to cure someone who was sick.

You can make your own pouch for treasures you collect.

To make a large pouch, find a piece of material that you like (felt works well). Cut a piece about 8" x 20" (20 cm x 50 cm). Fold up one narrow end about two-thirds of the way. Sew along the edge and then turn the material inside out. Decorate with beads or by painting (see symbols on page 75 for ideas). The leftover flap will tuck into your waistband.

A small pouch can be made by cutting a piece of material about 5" x 12" (12.5 cm x 30 cm). Sew up the edges and decorate. Attach with yarn or a strip of leather and hang around your neck.

Be sure to keep your pouch on you at all times, unless it is safely put away. If the rest of your group is willing, you can hold a special ceremony to share the contents of your pouches.

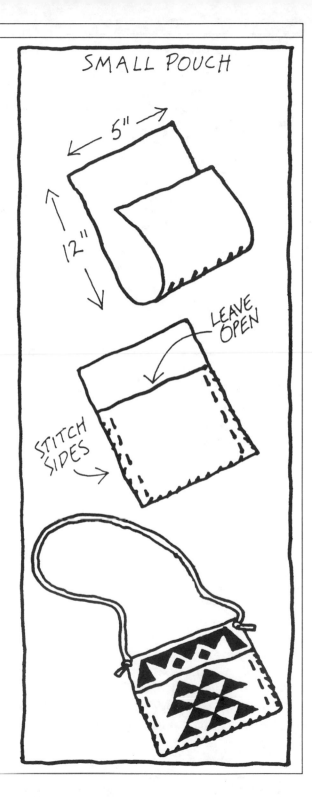

SMALL POUCH

5"

12"

LEAVE OPEN

STITCH SIDES

GAMES

Native American food

Corn, squash, wild rice, and beans were the staples of Native American diets. All these foods are considered to be tasty and healthful and can be found in any supermarket today! (To make wild rice, simply boil it until it is soft enough to eat.)

Corn was considered to be sacred food by most Native Americans. And they should know — they invented popcorn! They cooked over an open fire, in clay pots filled with sand. When the corn popped it rose up to the top for easy eating.

Pebble game

To play, all you need is a small pebble the size of a marble. Two players sit facing each other. The player with the pebble passes it from one hand to the other, all the while singing, either well or terribly, or even purposely terribly. The other player is supposed to keep his eyes on the pebble, though the pebble passer tries to break his concentration. When the player with the pebble is ready, he holds both hands out in front of him, his fingers closed.

Now the player without the pebble must guess which hand holds the pebble. If he guesses right, he gets the pebble. If he guesses wrong, the pebble passer tries to trick him again! The game can be played very fast.

Rooster balance game

Another favorite is the funny rooster game. In this game, two players play inside a circle, about 8' (2.5 m) in diameter. The players squat down so their knees touch their chests, and hold their arms like chicken wings, hands tucked inside their armpits.

The object of the game is to chase your opponent out of the circle, while still staying on your feet. It's not easy!

DANCES

AFTER SUNDOWN

After sundown is the time for stories. Native Americans have a strong tradition of story-telling. They use as much verbal magic and acting ability as they can in the telling of every tale. You can find books with some tales at the library. Ask the librarian to help you. Read them and pick a story out. Once you know the story you are going to tell, put the book away. After sundown, re-tell the tale using all the drama you can muster. Many of the stories feature talking animals. Be sure you give each character a different "voice" in your story. If each camper learns just one story, there will be more to share and enjoy.

American Indians danced to express their deepest feelings, whether it was fear before a battle or the sheer joy of living.

The Crow Fair Powwow

The powwow dance is a happy dance done to express gratitude for anything good that has happened, from the birth of a child to a celebration of good weather. Today, Native Americans gather each summer on the Crow Reservation in Montana for the Crow Fair, the largest powwow in North America. After a big opening parade, the dance begins. The adults and children dance in four groups — Traditional, Fancy, Grass, and Jingle-dress. The dancers' clothing may reflect a certain tribe, such as the floral pattern of the Woodland Indians, or represent a close relationship with nature by using eagle feathers, shells, and horsehair as decoration. The Jingle-dress dance is based on the story of Ojibwa, whose daughter was very sick. He dreamed that if she danced in a dress made with one shell for each day of the year, she would get well. When he woke up, Ojibwa made the dress and asked his daughter to dance in it. When she did, she was cured. Today, the Jingle-dress dancers have tin cones, instead of shells, on their dresses, that make pretty tinkling sounds during the dance.

SKY WATCH Here Comes The Sun

MAKE A SUNDIAL

*Let others talk of rain and showers,
I count only sunny hours!*

SUNDIAL SAYING

You can make a sundial that will tell the time on a sunny day, even if you aren't anywhere near a clock or watch! Here are two simple designs that can be made over the course of a sunny weekend. One is for a permanent sundial; the other is for a portable model.

A handmade clock

To make a permanent sundial, find a plate or shallow bowl that is not being used. An old wooden bowl is perfect.

Glue the flat edge of a wooden chopstick in a standing position in the exact center of the bowl or plate. If you are using a shallow bowl, you may have to pool some glue in the center to hold the stick. In that case, let the glue sit for at least an hour to thicken before you insert the chopstick. Support with toothpicks overnight.

Use a pencil to lightly outline each hour. (More on marking hours below.)

To paint a permanent sundial, fill in the spaces between your pencil marks with fine brushes and long lasting paint. *Let the artist in you come to play.* You are not just making a tool, but a fine timepiece!

You may want to add a sundial saying around the bowl. Small letter stencils work well, and so does dry alphabet soup!

If you are working with a plate, find one with a subdued design. You can cut the hour numerals from bits of vinyl, suede, or leather, and glue them onto the plate. With permission, you can cut large, black numerals from magazines and paint them over with clear nail polish. Sequins are a nice addition, too.

A portable sundial

To make the portable sundial model, you'll need a ball point pen, a piece of cardboard (white is best), markers and chalk, an alarm clock, and a place that is sunny all day.

Get your materials together, and draw a circle on the paper, with an X in the very middle. This will be where you hold the ball point pen to tell time after the dial is made.

To use your sundial away from home, carry the ball point pen and the paper, and stand in a sunny place. When you place the pen on the X, you'll know the time by where the shadow falls.

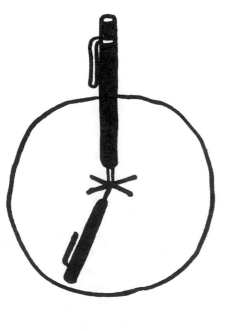

Marking hours on your sundial

Take the base of your sundial, whether it's a plate, a bowl, or paper, to a sunny place, with no trees or buildings nearby. Outline the ground around the base with chalk or string so that you'll be able to put it in exactly the same spot later on.

Next, set an alarm for five minutes before whatever hour you want to begin marking. Use both days of the weekend to fill in the hours.

When the alarm rings, go outside and put the paper in the space you marked. Use a ball point pen to mark the paper sundial, or a light pencil for the permanent model. Outline the shape that the shadow of the stick or vertical pen makes. Write or note the hour inside the shape.

Do this for every hour of daylight. The shadows will vary in length, making an attractive pattern on your dial.

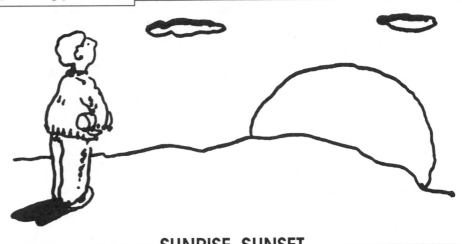

SUNRISE, SUNSET

During the same day, it's fun to experience both sunrise and sunset. Think of the best place you can go to witness these daily but dramatic miracles. Is there a hill near your home with a good view of the sky?

At dawn, carry a thermos filled with something wonderful, as well as a sweater or jacket. Daybreak can be a chilly time of day. Then, get comfortable and enjoy the spectacular. Never look directly at the sun — it could hurt your eyes. It's the sky around the sun that can take your breath away.

That evening, arrange to gather before dark to make a return trip. This time you'll watch the sun disappear over the other side of the planet.

MAKE A SOLAR SYSTEM SALAD

This salad isn't quite for eating — well, not at first anyway. Its purpose is to show the relative sizes of the planets in our solar system.

Mercury = A green pea

Venus = A round, unshelled walnut

Earth = A small onion, close to the size of the walnut. (For the moon, half of a dry lentil bean)

Mars = A plump, red cherry

Jupiter = A 9" (22.5 cm) head of lettuce

Saturn = A grapefruit

Uranus = A 8" (20 cm) cabbage

Neptune = A big orange

Pluto = A peppercorn

The Sun is too big to put into this salad! If you put it in this equation, it would be as big as an apartment building!

You can lay the salad out in the same relationship that the real planets are in, too. But you'll need some room to do it! The universe is a pretty big place, even when you scale it way, way down!

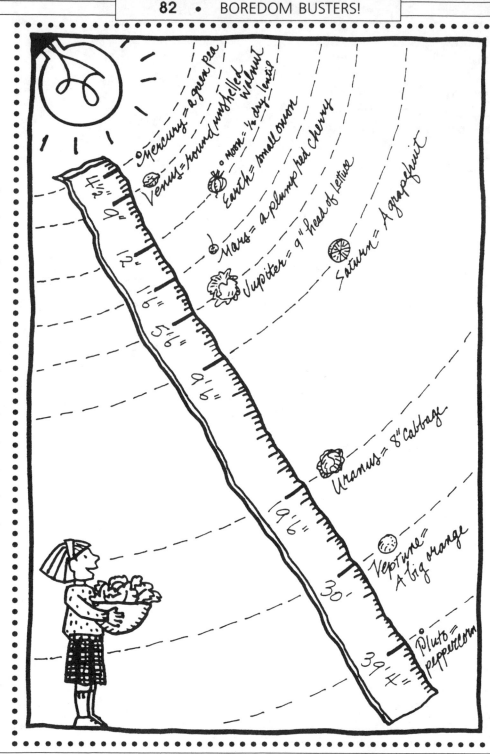

How it's done

In the real solar system, Earth is over 92 million miles (14 billion km) from the sun. Whew! Quite a trip! Let's call that distance our basic unit of measurement, and represent it by one foot. Then, put the other planets in relation to the sun and Earth.

If the distance from the Earth to the Sun is one foot, then:

Mercury would be about 4 1/2" (11 cm) from the sun

Venus would be 9" (22.5 cm)

Earth would be 1' (30 cm)

Mars — a foot and a half (45 cm)

Jupiter — 5' 6" (2 m)

Saturn — 9' 6" (3 m)

Uranus — 19' 6" (6 m)

Neptune — 30' (9.5 m)

Pluto — 39' 4" (12.5 m)

Notice the big skip from Neptune to Uranus?

It's fun to measure these distances in your backyard with a yardstick. Or, another way to go is to convert them all to one-inch scale. If the distance of Earth to the sun were one inch (2.5 cm), how far away would Pluto be?

Weather Watch

By scanning the sky for colors and other clues, people have tried to predict the weather since time began. Test these bits of ancient meteorology to see if they are really true:

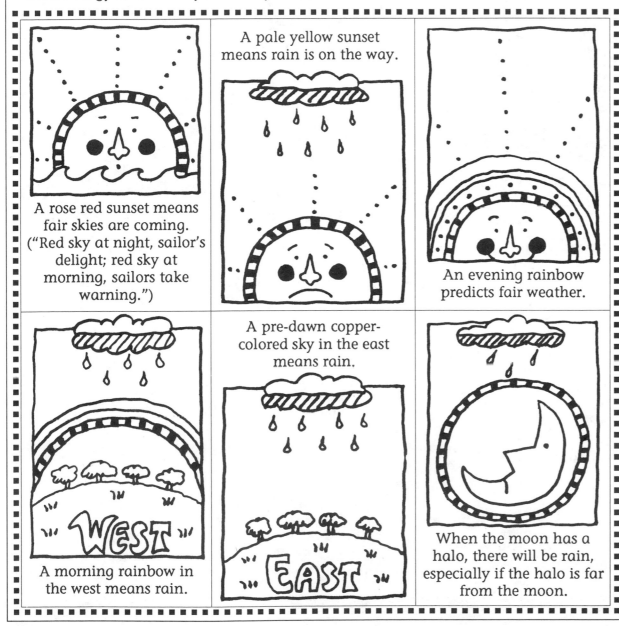

A rose red sunset means fair skies are coming. ("Red sky at night, sailor's delight; red sky at morning, sailors take warning.")

A pale yellow sunset means rain is on the way.

An evening rainbow predicts fair weather.

A morning rainbow in the west means rain.

A pre-dawn copper-colored sky in the east means rain.

When the moon has a halo, there will be rain, especially if the halo is far from the moon.

The Sun warms the Earth, the Earth warms the air

You can fight global warming. Global warming happens when the earth gets hot and heats up air around our planet. What makes air hot? Burning fossil fuels, like oil and gas, and also certain substances we've used for refrigeration.

Many scientists believe that global warming is a serious danger for our planet. If the polar ice caps melt, there may be flooding. Some farmlands might become deserts from too much heat.

But there are things we all can do that will help stop global warming! The most important one is to use energy wisely. Don't drive someplace if you can easily bike there. Turn off lights when you're not using them. Don't use air-conditioning if you don't have to. Plant trees when you can. Let government officials know what you want.

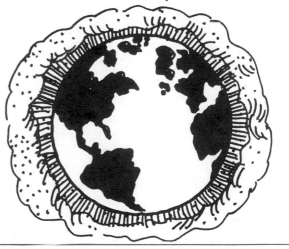

SOMETHING TRULY AWESOME

When you go outside on a clear night and look up at the starry sky, you're doing something people have done since time began. As you look up, pause for a moment to realize that you are standing on a tiny sphere that is just like those pin-points of light up there. The Earth, which seems so solid to us, is really floating in the vastness of space, surrounded by the blackness, just like those stars.

ANCIENT WISDOM AND WANDERING STARS

*L*ong ago, the average person knew more about the sky than most of us do today. After all, a lonely shepherd tending his flock didn't have a TV to make the night pass faster. What he did have, though, was the greatest show of all — the starry night sky.

Night after night, looking up at the heavens, ancient people noticed things. They saw that many stars seemed to travel in groups or patterns. They called these patterns *constellations* and made up stories about them.

Other stars seemed to be lone travelers. They'd appear dependably at certain times or seasons, but they didn't seem to be part of any constellation. The ancient people called them *wandering stars.* Now we know that they are really *planets* of our own *solar system*, orbiting around the sun the same way Earth does.

Which way is up?

Knowing the stars helped ancient people get around, too. If someone knew where a certain star was, he'd never have to fear getting lost. Because the ancient people knew the night sky, they were able to find North, South, East and West without the help of a compass. The same can be true for you, too! Keep reading.

What is a star?

A star is a mass of burning gases. That's what makes them shine. The star we know best, of course, is our very own *sun*. At a mere 93 million miles away, it's closer to us than any other star in the sky. The stars we see twinkling at night are much, much farther away.

Star light — how bright?

The brightness of stars is measured by *magnitude*. The lower the magnitude, the brighter the star. For instance, zero is the brightest, and five is the dimmest.

GETTING TO KNOW YOU

Stars are kind of like people. There may be a lot of them, but the best way to get to know them is a few at a time! If you were sent to a new school, and walked into a room filled with a bunch of kids you didn't know, it might make you feel uncomfortable. Make friends with just one or two of those kids, though, and your experience would soon change. Your new friends would introduce you to others, and soon you'd have a whole pack of friends.

Well, it's the same with stars. Getting to know one or two will introduce you to the whole sky!

Into the night

Human eyes can adjust to many different light conditions, which makes them perfect for stargazing. When you go out to explore the night sky, try this experiment.

Walk outside from a brightly lit house, then look up to see how many stars you see. Next, close your eyes for a full five minutes. When you open them again you will see many more stars than before. The sky didn't change. Your eyes did. Adjusting for lower light, the center part — your pupils — enlarged and let you see more. After half an hour in the dark, your pupils will be completely open.

A night when the moon is a small crescent is best for stargazing, but you'll be able to see stars any night that the sky is clear. If you live in the city, close to bright street lights, go to the darkest place you can find.

What to take along

You may want to take a star chart and a flashlight along on your night sky explores. A star chart is a map of the sky that tells exactly which constellations and planets are visible on any given night. Most newspapers publish sky charts in their weather sections. If your paper doesn't, pick up a book at the library that has the same information.

If you bring a flashlight, be sure to cover the lens with red cellophane, or paint it with red nail polish. That way your eyes won't be tricked into adjusting for brighter light everytime you look at the chart.

The following items aren't really necessary for stargazing, but they sure don't hurt:

A thermos filled with something wonderful: lemonade on a hot night, hot chocolate on a cool one.

Friends or family. When it comes to searching the skies for constellations, four, six, eight or ten eyes are definitely better than two.

HI, I'M POLARIS, THE NORTH STAR. WHAT'S YOUR NAME?

If you like having a friend you can depend on, you'll like *Polaris*, the *North Star*. This star, which is sometimes called the Pole Star, is the only one whose position never seems to change. Night after night, season after season, you will find Polaris in exactly the same spot in the sky that it was the night before. That's because it's located over the North Pole. While Earth twirls and spins through space, the North Star seems to remain steadfast, fixed in its place. And where exactly is its place? You guessed it. In the North.

Polaris may not be the brightest star in the sky, but its dependability makes it one of the most important. This is the star that can tell you which direction is which. It's also the friend who can introduce you to other friends!

Two ways to find polaris

FIND THE BIG DIPPER

The *Big Dipper* is one of the easiest constellations to find because of its distinctive shape: like a large, old-fashioned soup ladle with a square-shaped bowl. The handle of the Big Dipper has two bright stars called pointers. These point to Polaris. When you've found the Big Dipper, draw an imaginary line through the *pointers* to the next bright star. That's Polaris.

FIND THE LITTLE DIPPER

If you're already facing North, your eyes may come across the *Little Dipper*. The Little Dipper is smaller and not as bright as the Big Dipper, but it, too, is in the shape of a squarish ladle. Polaris is the last star on the Little Dipper's handle.

East is East and West is West

Once you're able to find the North Star, you'll always know how to find East, West or South. *When you face Polaris, you're facing North. Left of you is West, and right of you is East. South will be behind you.*

AN UMBRELLA PLANETARIUM

You can make your own planetarium from an old black or navy blue umbrella by attaching star stickers onto the inside of the umbrella. Pretend that the place where the handle meets the top is Polaris, the North Star. Stick, tape, or glue on the star groups nearest the North Star. These are: The famous Big and Little Dippers; long, lovely Draco, the Dragon; Cepheus the King, with his pointy dunce cap; Cassiopeia, his queen, with her W-shaped crown; and the dim Giraffe. Make the stars from ready-made stickers, or cut them out of silver foil.

Ask a friend to hold your umbrella steadfast while you twirl under it. If you keep looking at the stars you've pasted inside the umbrella, they will seem to move!

ORION

Orion is one of the brightest winter constellations. The best time to view it is from December to March. Look out at the sky, facing south. The Orion constellation has seven main stars, including two very bright ones — Betelgeuse (pronounced Bet-el-jooz) and Rigel. Close to Orion is one of the brightest stars in the whole sky, Sirius, which is also called the Dog Star.

The Orion constellation is named after an ancient hero of Greek myth. You can tell the story to your star-gazing friends.

The Story of Orion

Orion was a hunter, and a very big one, as big as a giant! Wherever he traveled, he took his dog, Sirius. One day, Orion was walking through the forest with Sirius, when he saw seven beautiful sisters picking berries. Hoping that he could meet and marry one, Orion ran toward the girls.

When the seven sisters saw the giant racing toward them, they became frightened. They called to Zeus, the king of the gods, for help. Zeus turned the girls into seven pretty birds, who flew off right away, leaving poor Orion all alone again.

He is still up in the sky, roaming the forests with his faithful dog, looking for someone to love.

MAKE UP YOUR OWN CONSTELLATION STORY

Once you've found the Big and Little Dippers, you will soon be able to find Draco, the Dragon. The dragon's tail is between the dippers.

You can make up your own story about Draco. Maybe it's about the day he was very thirsty and wanted to drink from the Big Dipper . . . .

Better yet, design a new sky!

Ancient people made up stories about certain groups of stars, and so can *you*! You can create your own constellations! Trace the chart of the stars that travel around the North Pole (see page 86) to use as the beginning of a dot-to-dot picture (maybe we should call it a star-to-star picture).

Don't trace the connecting lines, though. Use a pencil to connect the dots of the stars the way you want them to be!

Constellations can be anything — animals, people, things — real or imagined.

Once you've created a picture, make up a story about it. If you do, you will be doing what people did six thousand years ago!

You can trace fresh dot-to-dot pages for your family or friends to create with. It's fun to compare the different stories that people will make up, based on the same stars of the night sky.

Shooting Stars

Have you ever seen a streak of light flash through the night sky? Then you've seen a shooting star! Of course, by the time you could point it out to a friend, it was probably gone.

Shooting stars are actually meteors. They are small pieces of rock or ash that are floating around the Earth. Some are large — large enough to make a hole when they crash into the Earth. But most are small — so small that they break apart into almost nothing by the time they land.

The light of a meteor comes from rubbing against the air on the way down.

You can see shooting or falling stars almost any night if you look in the sky long enough. Some people say that wishing on a falling star gets the best results of all!

The Evening and Morning Stars

Surprise! The *Evening Star* and the *Morning Star* are really the same thing! Not only that, it's not a star at all — it's the planet *Venus*!

Oh, well, despite the confusion, gazing at Venus is still a wonderful thing to do. This shining, silvery planet is one of the loveliest sights of the night sky.

The reason Venus is called the Morning or Evening star is that it only appears within three hours of sunset or sunrise. Look for Venus at twilight in the west; before dawn, it will be in the east. It is the brightest object in the sky, except for the sun and the moon.

Songs for stargazers

While you're lying on your blanket looking up at the sky, it's fun to think of all the songs you know with the words Sun, Moon, and Star, in them. How many can you think of?

Hello, down there!

Since Earth is round, and spinning in space, you are really looking up, down, over, across, and out when you look at the stars — not just up! It's fun to remember that when you stargaze.

☆ The average person can see about 2,000 stars on a clear night.

☆ The brightest star of summer is Vega, a bluish white star in the constellation Lyre. You can find Vega by finding Draco, the Dragon. Follow the tip of the dragon's head to the brightest star you see. That's Vega. Since our galaxy is moving through space, the stars change positions over time. Stick around about 12,000 years, and you'll find that Vega has become the new Pole Star!

☆ Before the days of eye charts, the little star Alcor, which sits close to Mizar (MY-zar), the second star down on the Big Dipper's handle, was used to test people's eyesight. If a person could see Alcor, it meant she had good eyesight. Can you spot this little star?

☆ The five brightest stars visible in North America:

Sirius — in Big Dog — bluish

Vega — in Lyre — bluish white

Capella — in Charioteer — yellowish

Arcturus — in Herdsman — orange

Rigel — in Orion — bluish white

American Indians called stars the Eyes of the Night Sky.

GROW YOUR OWN

Make a Terrarium

Terrarium is a big word, and it has an even bigger meaning. It means "a place of earth." A terrarium is a living, breathing place of Earth that you can create and bring into your house. It is also a wonderful gift to give.

HOW IT ALL STARTED

The first terrarium was created completely by accident! In 1829, an Englishman named Nathaniel Ward was trying to hatch a sphynx moth. He found a cocoon, put it in a glass jar with some soil, and closed the jar. A few days later something strange and wonderful happened. A small fern began sprouting inside the jar!

As the weeks went by, Ward noticed that his little fern was flourishing in its sealed world. How could it be?

This incredible incident encouraged Ward to begin experimenting with other kinds of plant life in enclosed environments. He learned how to grow all sorts of plants inside jars and glass cases. He called these new and beautiful inventions *terrariums*.

P.S. His orginal fern lived for over forty years!

Amazing but true

How could Ward's fern live in a completely sealed container? Don't plants need air and water in order to be healthy? Don't they need food?

The answer, of course, is yes. Plants need all those things. But amazingly, life inside a terrarium has them all!

The secret is that a terrarium is a small, but actual, living *ecosystem*. In it, there is everything a plant needs for a healthy and long life.

The air, or atmosphere, that the plant needs is provided by the air inside the container. The plants breathe in carbon dioxide, and breathe out oxygen, replenishing the atmosphere.

Light shining through the terrarium wall provides the power source that keeps the engine of life running. By a process called *photosynthesis*, plants convert light into energy to live, replenishing the carbon dioxide.

Water comes from the moisture in the soil, This water is recycled inside the container. It goes from the soil, to the air, and back again, over and over.

Food comes from the soil. In time, leaves that wither and fall, decompose. These provide food for the roots of the plant, thanks to the microscopic life in the soil, which helps break down the dead matter. It's good to have an earthworm in there, also, even though you won't see him much. (Worms shun the light.)

Food, water, air, and energy — a terrarium has all the conditions necessary for life.

Kinds of terrariums

Not all terrariums are completely sealed for all time. Some are closed on a part-time basis. These can be opened from time to time, to allow people access for trimming or pruning the plants, or giving them an occasional spritz of water.

Some terrariums are open all the time to accommodate more sun, though these have to be watered regularly.

Others, sometimes called *vivariums*, have small animals in them, in addition to the microscopic creatures and occasional worm found in all healthy soil.

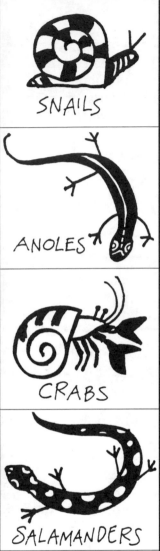

SNAILS

ANOLES

CRABS

SALAMANDERS

TURTLES

ANIMALS LIVE IN TERRARIUMS, TOO

Snails, anoles, some crabs, and salamanders can live out their entire life spans in vivariums. These little creatures won't need any special tending or feeding either, if the system has been set up with their needs in mind.

Tiny turtles are good vivarium dwellers, too. These miniature amphibians only need an occasional morsel of food to thrive quite happily inside their terrarium homes.

Dryland hermit crabs are actually helpful citizens in their terrariums. These comical little animals keep their homes clean by munching on debris. They never damage any plants or interfere with other life in the case, either.

If you decide to create a vivarium of your own, follow the rules for making a terrarium. But remember, a vivarium needs to be considerably larger than a terrarium. To support animal life it should be at least 2' x 1' (60 cm x 30 cm). A large aquarium makes an ideal place for a vivarium.

A healthy interplay between light, soil, water, plants and creatures is the very stuff of life. Bring them all together and the result is real life!

AN ECOSYSTEM OF YOUR VERY OWN

Creating a terrarium is a lot of fun. You'll have to get a few simple things together and make a field trip out to the wild (or maybe your own backyard). Then, as your reward, you get to put it all together to create your own lovely, living "place of Earth."

The right container

Start by collecting one or more containers. Clean peanut butter or pickle jars make good terrariums, and so do any other clear, wide-mouthed containers made of see-thru plastic or glass.

Large brandy snifters, glass aquariums, and bell jars — the glass-domed containers used to store cakes — are also candidates for terrarium cases. It doesn't matter whether the plants go inside or under the glass. What matters is that there's a self-supporting ecosystem inside.

It's even possible to build a terrarium in a narrow-necked bottle, like a large cider jug. The result is like a ship in the bottle, and just as impressive. Naturally, this kind of terrarium takes longer to create, so it may not be the best choice for your first project. Garden shops don't sell tools for gardening inside bottles, so you'd have to invent your own, from wire hangers, long tweezers, or whatever else you can think of that might work.

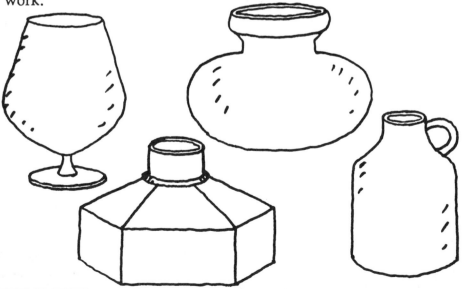

To make your terrarium

You need:
A terrarium
container
(improvised)

Small stones or gravel

Activated filter carbon
(or charcoal)

Healthy soil

A very small
piece of sponge
(optional)

A piece of screen
(or mesh or
hardware cloth)

Plants, or moss

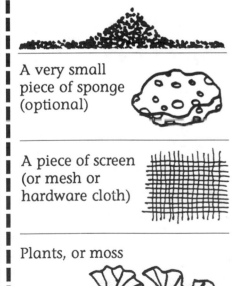

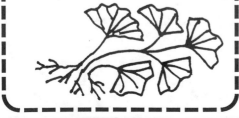

Time for a field trip

Once you've got the materials together, you're ready to make a field trip to collect the plants that will live inside your terrarium.

Depending on the terrain where you live, you'll have different choices to make about what to include.

If you live in a hot dry climate like Arizona, you may choose sand and desert plants for your terrarium. Because of their unusual needs for strong sun, you may choose to leave your terrarium open.

Someone from the Northeast might collect different kinds of mosses and lichen to place in the terrarium.

No matter where you live, experiment with different combinations of plants to find out which work best together.

Whether you're selecting plants from the forest floor, a marshland, or a desert, keep in mind the size of the specimens you find. With terrariums, bigger is definitely not better. Miniature plants, the smallest you can find, have special charm when viewed from a terrarium window. And best of all, they won't soon outgrow their new home away from home. Tiny plants that grow in shady spots make ideal terrarium occupants.

As you collect your plant life, make sure that nothing is on your state's endangered species list (call your state environmental protection agency if you're unsure about any plant). And take only a small portion of any kind you find. Leave at least four-fifths of any given plant grouping. If you're on private property, you'll need permission from the owners before you collect the plants. But most people will give their approval happily once you assure them that you will only need a small piece of earth.

When you've selected the particular plant or piece of earth you like, dig deeply around and under it. It's important to include the root system of the plant you want, so dig deeply. When the soil is loosened, lift the plants gently — by the leaves, not the stem. Never pluck a plant or tug at its roots. If the piece of earth you're collecting doesn't lift out easily, dig under it some more, and try again.

Because you are collecting only a small portion of any given green spot, you can be confident that the small hole you've just made will be filled within a matter of weeks. Tap the ground gently when you're finished, though, and cover any exposed roots of the plants that won't be coming home with you.

Place the specimens you've collected in a zip-lock bag filled with a breath of air for special cushioning.

A firm foundation

Once you're back from the field trip, it's time to start assembling your terrarium. This is done from the bottom up.

First, place a loose layer of gravel on the terrarium floor. Then sprinkle a small amount of activated charcoal on it. Activated charcoal will help keep your ecosystem free of fungi. You can buy it at any pet store. Plain charcoal will work, too.

Now cover the gravel with a small piece of plastic screening that has a slit in the middle. (If you don't have a plastic screen, try cloth mesh, hardware cloth, or other improvised material.) On top of that, put a thin layer of healthy soil. The screen will prevent the soil from sinking all the way into the gravel. In order for water, air, and nutrients to move freely, soil inside the terrarium shouldn't be packed too tightly.

If you want, you can slice a piece of sponge or foam rubber (no more than 1/3" [8 mm] wide). Insert this into a slit in the screen. Leave most of it standing so it can be covered by soil. The sponge will act like a candle wick, bringing water from the bottom of the terrarium up to the plant roots.

When the sponge is in place, you're ready to assemble your very own forest floor.

You can make a simple, flat floor by pouring soil over the mesh and the sponge. Or, you can try using stones to create a terraced look, complete with minature rock ledges. If you decide to make different levels, be sure that all the soil inside is interconnected, throughout the whole terrarium. An island of soil, separated by rocks from the other soil in the terrarium, won't receive the food it needs to flourish.

Once the floor is assembled, you're ready to place the plants and mosses you've collected into the terrarium. Gently spread and cover their roots, lightly tapping down the soil as you plant. Here is where your sense of creativity can come into play. Arrange the plants artfully, in any way that you wish. You may want to add a small ceramic figure, or special stones as decoration.

When you're finished, give your new creation a healthy spritz of water, and cover it.

PLANTS

ROCK

CERAMIC FIGURE

HEALTHY SOIL

SCREEN

CHARCOAL
SPONGE
GRAVEL

SAY HELLO TO TERRY

Your terrarium may look a little scraggly at first. Like most brand new living creatures, it may need some time to fill out and grow into its new surroundings. In just a week or two, the plants inside will have become more comfortable in their new home and have found the best way to turn to their light source.

Unless you are working with sun-loving plants, avoid keeping your terrarium in direct sunlight. Filtered light or shade is best for most terrarium plants during most of the year. On the coldest days of winter, you might want to give your terrarium a treat by placing it in direct sunlight for an hour or two, but as a rule, keep your terrarium in a place where it will receive light, but not direct rays of sunlight.

The terrarium you've created won't need very much care from you, maybe none! You'll want to check in on it from time to time, though. Some like an occasional spritz of water, others need to have a trimming now and then. And like all living things, your terrarium will enjoy some love and appreciation, too!

In putting together a terrarium, you will have created a small, but real — and *living* — ecosystem. Hey! You must be a very powerful person!

Team up with Mother Nature

When you plant a garden, you get to work with one of the all time greats — Mother Nature herself! Whether you're creating a window box, or a mini-farm, the process is always the same:

Mother N. provides the basics — the soil, sun, and some water. Your job is planting and caretaking, or puttering. You'll take on the jobs of inspector, looking for weeds or pests, and part-time parent, giving water, food, and encouragement to the plants you're growing.

If you and Mother N. both do your jobs — and you know *she* will — look for dynamite results! The product of your partnership will pop right out of the soil and grow! You'll have beautiful flowers to enjoy and tasty food to eat.

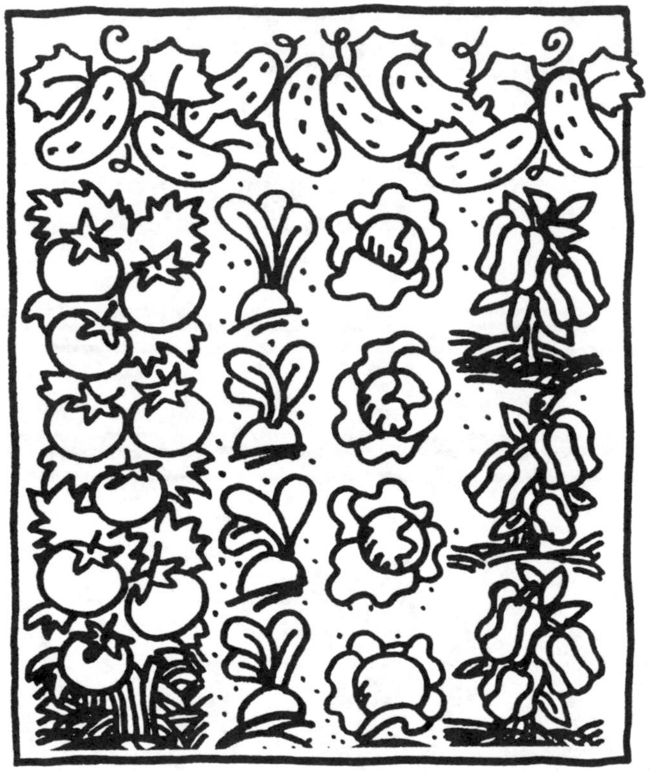

Give fools their gold and knaves their power,
Let fortune's bubbles rise and fall,
Who sows a field or trains a flower or plants a tree,
Is more than all.

JOHN GREENLEAF WHITTIER

EASY AS ONE, TWO, THREE — GETTING THE BASICS DOWN

Soil, sun and *water* — those are the big three when it comes to gardening success. No matter what you plant, or where, you need all three to make your garden grow. Before you get down to creating a garden, bone up on these basics. When you're enjoying the flowers and food you've grown, you'll be glad you did.

PLAIN OLD DIRT?

Talk about taking something for granted! Think about soil. All our lives, we walk on it, run on it, hop, skip, and jump on it. We play on it, sit on it, stomp on it. But do we *appreciate* it? Not usually!

Getting to know you

Reach down and take a handful of soil. How does it feel? Smell it. If it's healthy soil, you'll be sniffing a clean, woodsy aroma. Spread the soil out on a piece of white paper. If you have a magnifying glass, take a closer look. What's in the soil?

A handful of healthy soil contains far more than you'd imagine. First of all, there are those millions of tiny microbes, along with the air and water they (and we) need in order to live. Good soil also contains minerals that are recycled over and over — from earth, to plants, to birds, to animals, and back.

Unhealthy soil is useless in a garden. No matter how many seeds you plant in it, and no matter how much you water them, they will fail to thrive. Some won't even sprout. Others may grow, but they'll always be sickly.

Making good soil

You can help your garden soil to be healthy by adding *organic* matter to it. Organic is another word for living. And where can you get organic matter for your garden? From your garbage! That old banana peel may not be much use to you, but for the microbes in your garden soil, it will be a feast!

When organic matter breaks down, it becomes rich soil called *compost* (or *humus*). Making compost is easy, but it does take some time. If you don't already have a *compost heap* on your property, start one now. Then you'll be sure to have rich garden soil the next time you plant.

GRASS CLIPPINGS

BIODEGRADEABLE GARBAGE

LEAVES

YOU ARE THE SUNSHINE OF MY LIFE

INDOOR GARDENERS

For you, picking a garden spot is easy. Put your plants in the sunniest place in the house. If you don't have sun, see below.

OUTDOOR GARDENERS

Go outside and notice where your property has sun and where it has shade. Walk around in the morning, at noon, and at different times of day to get a good sense of how much sun different places get.

Here comes the sun!

If you have a sunny spot for a garden, you're in luck! The vast majority of flowers love sun. As for vegetables, they won't produce without a full six hours a day of those golden rays! With a sunny garden spot, you can choose many different plants and flowers to grow in your garden.

Part sun, part shade

If you have some sun, but not a lot — at least two hours a day, you can still grow flowers, and even a few plants to eat, like *carrots*, *lettuce*, and some herbs, like curly *parsley*. These delicious plants look pretty growing alongside flowers, too.

When all you've got is shade

A shady garden may not produce all the food and flowers you'd like to grow, but if you plant the right things in it, you can have a lovely and successful garden under the trees.

Among the best shade-loving flowers are Impatiens. These low-growing, bushy plants each have dozens of flowers on them — flowers that bloom from spring through fall. Not only that, they come in lots of colors — purple, pink, orange, salmon, red, and white.

When you plant your Impatiens, remember to leave about eight inches between the plants. Before you know it, the little seedlings you brought home from the garden shop will grow and spread out — so they'll need room.

A shady farm?

The world of easy-to-grow, shade-loving vegetables is very very small. You may have luck growing, lettuce, though. It looks good next to flowers, and it's delicious, too.

WATER TO THRIVE ON

Now that you know how to make healthy soil, and you've found a good place to plant, your next (and ongoing) job as Mother Nature's helper is to give your plants the right amount of water to drink.

OUTDOOR GARDENERS

Mother Nature will provide some rainwater, but it's up to you to make sure your plants get the water they need to thrive. Water them in the early morning, or better yet, in the late afternoon. Watering at noon, when it's hot, wastes water.

When you water, make sure you give your plants a *good long drink*, one that will really soak their roots. Twice a week should be often enough, if you're doing it right. Overwatering plants doesn't do them any good.

INDOOR (AND WINDOW BOX) GARDENERS

You'll have to water more frequently, three or four times a week and maybe even every day in hot weather. Follow the guidelines for outdoor gardeners, giving your plants a good soaking when you water.

THE BIG DAY IS HERE!

You know how to make soil healthy, and how to pick a garden site. All you have to do now is choose what you're planting, and plant! Once you've decided, go to it — and good luck!

INDOOR GARDENERS

It's time to prepare your window box and flower pots. You can plant in all sorts of containers — cans, jelly jars, gallon milk jugs cut off at the top, mugs, wooden boxes, or buckets. Decorate with stickers to cover old labels, or look for pretty cans to start with.

Prick a couple of small holes in the bottom of your planter, if possible, and add an inch or two (2.5 cm or 5 cm) of pebbles for drainage. Fill with healthy soil, and you're ready to plant!

OUTDOOR GARDENERS

When you've chosen your garden site, prepare the soil by turning it over with a spade (or trowel or spoon, depending on what you have). If you get lumps or clods in the soil, break them up with a hoe, or the edge of your spade. Newly prepared garden soil should be crumbly, not clumpy. Take out any big sticks or rocks. Pull out any small tree roots. Add some compost or potting soil.

Soil that's ready to plant looks a little like the dry ingredients of a chocolate cake mix. Smooth it out with a rake, and you're ready to plant!

PLANTING

This part is pretty easy. If you are planting seeds, just follow the directions on the package. Make a hole for the seed with your finger or with a stick. Indoor gardeners, use a pencil.

We recommend getting some *seedlings* as well, though. Waiting for plants to grow is more fun when something is already started.

To plant a seedling, dig a hole as deep, or somewhat deeper, than the roots of the seedling. Wet the hole and wait for the water to seep at least half way down. Then gently remove the seedling from its package, without grabbing or squeezing it. Hold it gently by the leaves, not the stem, and set it into the hole. Fill around the roots with soil, and pat it down.

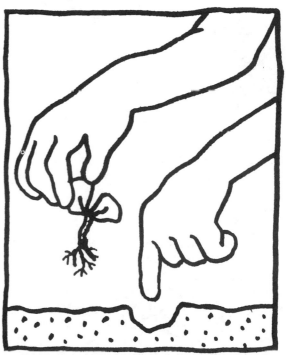

FOOD CROPS

Feeling hungry? How about planting some . . . .

Lettuce

Lettuce likes shade or some sun. Plant in Spring, and again in summer.

Beans

There are all kinds of beans to grow — string beans, wax beans, snap beans, pole beans, and others, too! Some need staking or a trellis, and some (called bush beans) don't; but all beans are easy to grow. The main thing to remember about them is to harvest them *before they grow too big.* Pick the young beans right off the vine or the bush for the best tasting beans.

Carrots

These slow growers need sun, but they can tolerate some shade. Their upper leaf is lacy and pretty; the carrot is the root of the plant.

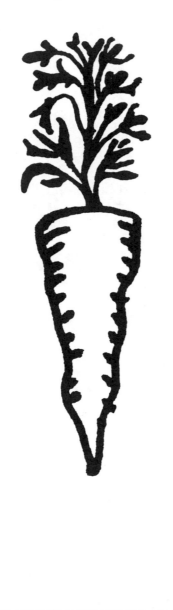

Tomatoes

Sun loving, all the way. They grow well in gardens or containers as long as they have plenty of sun. Start with seedlings for best results.

Don't be alarmed if your tomato plants look droopy the first week or so after they're planted. They'll perk up if they are getting the water, sun and care they need.

Many tomatoes grow on vines, and need a lot of space, so you may want to stake them.

INDOOR GARDENERS

Cherry tomatoes grow especially well in containers and window boxes.

Cucumbers

These crunchy cool veggies love water, so make sure they get plenty of it. If your soil is sandy, you're in luck. If your soil has more clay in it, build it up around the cuke's base so it holds water better for the plant. Never let a cucumber plant get bone dry.

Radishes

Here's the number one fastest grower in a vegetable garden!

A bucket of potatoes

Got a potato growing eyes in your refrigerator? Don't just stare at it. Cut off chunks with the eyes on them, and plant them in a bucket of good rich soil. Plant them fairly deep down (about 6 inches [15 cm]). They'll find their way up to the surface. After a while, a leafy potato plant will sprout in the soil. Water it and let it grow to about 18 inches (45 cm). Then harvest the potatoes by pulling out the plant. The potatoes will be attached to the roots. Or, you can plant your potatoes right in the garden.

Some people plant tomatoes right on top of their potatoes. Well, why not? The potato and tomato plants are in the same family. After you've harvested all your tomatoes, pull out the plants to get at your crop of potatoes.

Pumpkin patch

Pumpkins are native American vines, and they like the wide open spaces! Each one of them takes up *at least* a square yard! If you have a sunny spot for a pumpkin plant, dig a hole about 1 foot (30 cm) square. Fill with healthy soil; then add a mound on top. Pile on more healthy soil so the mound is at least 8 inches (20 cm) high.

Into the mound plant 3 to 5 pumpkin seeds, and keep them watered. They will sprout very quickly (in about a week). Choose the healthiest one or two sprouts to concentrate on, and discard the others.

After a while, male and female flowers will appear. You'll know which is which by the way they're shaped. The female has a bulb on the end; that's the part that will become a pumpkin — with a little help from you or a bee, that is.

If you don't have bees in your garden, use a soft brush to take some of the yellow dust from the male flower and gently brush it into the female flower. That's called *pollination*.

Once you've got three flowers on a stem, nip any others off. Nip off the fuzzy end of the vine, too, to make a bigger pumpkin.

The green bulb on the female flower will grow and grow. In time it will turn yellow, then orange. When the pumpkin is changing from green to yellow, you can write your name in it with a ball point pen. (Don't scratch it too hard, though.) Your pumpkin is now yours alone — you can prove it by the autograph that will grow into the pumpkin!

Pest alert!

Watch out for these two: mealybugs and aphids

Mealybugs are the tiny creatures that make white foam on plants. *Aphids* are tiny, stubby white bugs. These two creatures have the same bad habit. They like to hang out on the underside of plants, eating away!

To get rid of these pests, and others like them, use soap, not chemicals. Put 3 tablespoons (40 ml) of soap flakes or liquid into a bucket of water, and give the plants a refreshing shower.

Many gardners believe that if you plant marigolds near vegetables, it helps to cut down on garden pests. Plants helping other plants is called *companion planting.*

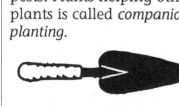

FLOWERS, FLOWERS, FLOWERS

You'll be making the world a more beautiful place when you plant flowers! Here are some that are easy to grow:

Oxe-Eyed Daisy, Shasta Daisy

They are easy-to-grow, sun-loving plants, but they can take some shade, too. Best of all, they'll grow again, year after year, once you've planted them.

Nasturtiums

These showy red and orange flowers grew wild in Peru. Now we can enjoy them in window boxes, containers, or a garden. They don't need much water, and they can also tolerate some shade.

Petunias

Petunias come in many different colors; some of them have flowers that are striped! Good in the garden or in window boxes.

Marigolds

Marigolds are hardy little flowers that bloom and bloom and bloom. Nip off the dead flowers, and you'll encourage new ones to grow.

Tickweed (or Coreopsis)

Birds will love your garden if you plant Tickweed. And you'll love the beautiful cut flowers you get. It's good for window boxes, too.

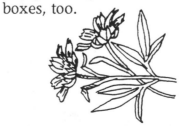

Geranium

Good for containers, window boxes, or a garden, as long as they get a good amount of sun. Water well. The flowers are big and beautiful.

Portulaca (also called Rose Moss)

Like Tickweed, birds love Portulaca. Portulaca needs a lot of sun, but just a regular amount of water.

Zinnias

Zinnias are bright, colorful flowers that make great bouquets.

MOTHER NATURE SENDS SOME HELP

If your garden soil is healthy, look for these assistants who will be able helpers, tending your plants:

The lowly earthworm

It's time this lowly worm got some respect! Day after day, he and his companions toil away, bringing air and water to the soil as they chew up the earth to burrow their little homes. Yet people call them gross and disgusting! It's not fair!

Ladybugs, butterflies, and bees

If you see any of these creatures hanging around your garden, make them feel welcome. Most butterflies, and all ladybugs, eat the bugs that eat our plants! As for bees, they help plants produce flowers and fruit, so don't shoo them away!

FEEDING YOUR GARDEN

If you've used manure or rich organic soil, you won't need to feed your garden. Your plants will get all the food they need right from the soil.

But if you want to give your plants some extra food now and then, here are some suggestions:

A gray water treat

Gray water may not sound appealing to you, but your plants will like it a lot. Gray water is another name for water that's already been used once, such as the water you cooked corn in or the water that your cut flowers lived in. This water has extra nourishment that plants love. Even soapy water is okay!

Wood ashes — yum, yum!

It's not our idea of a taste treat, and not yours either, but your garden plants will love a few ashes scattered around their roots! Ashes make great fertilizer.

Wondrous Crystal Gardens

Y ou can create a beautiful crystal garden that will grow and bloom over the weekend! Start on Friday for a beautiful display on Sunday. Growing crystals is easy and fun to do.

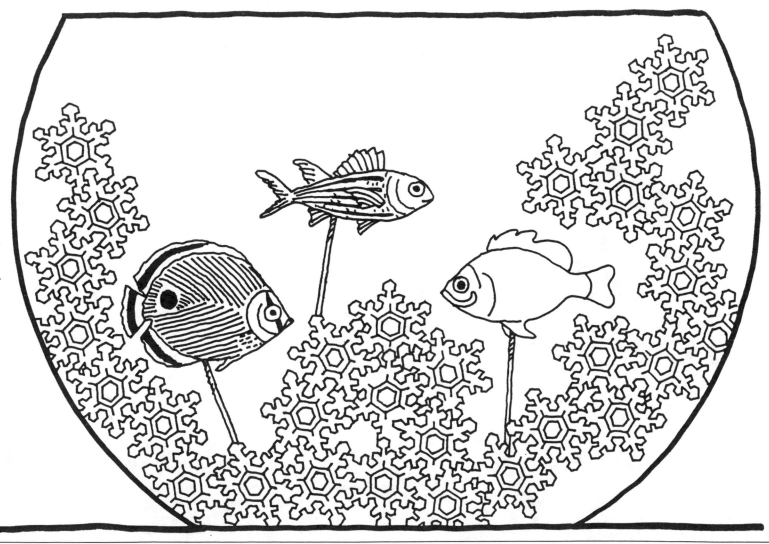

YOU'LL NEED:

A glass bowl

Food coloring

Some pieces of charcoal, porous brick, cement, or an old sponge

Regular table salt (iodized or uniodized, it doesn't matter)

A small amount of laundry bluing*

You can find laundry bluing in the laundry section of most supermarkets. It comes in a small blue bottle. If you have trouble finding it, write to Mrs. Stewart's Bluing, P.O. Box 201405, Bloomington, MN 55420.

To make your garden, put the charcoal (or whatever you are using to grow the crystals on) in a shallow, glass bowl. Pour or sprinkle two tablespoons (25 ml) each of water, salt, and laundry bluing over the base material. The next day, add two more tablespoons (25 ml) of salt.

On the third day, some crystals will already be growing. Pour two tablespoons (25 ml) each of salt, water, and bluing into the bottom of the bowl (not over the charcoal). Now you can add a few drops of food coloring to each piece of charcoal or brick.

Keep your crystal garden in a dry place where it can get air, and watch it bloom.

A DEEP-SEA CORAL GARDEN

Your crystal garden may remind you of coral growing in the sea. You can add to this effect by adding fish to the garden. Bend a few large paper clips so that they can stand on their own.

Three ways to make fish

1 You can draw some colorful fish on paper, using markers or crayons. Be sure to include dorsal fins and tails, for realistic detail. Tape to the standing end of the paper clips.

2 If you have some used nature magazines or catalogues, you might find pictures of real tropical fish. If so, glue the pictures onto cardboard, cut them out, and tape each one to a paper clip.

3 You can also sculpt fish from play clay (see page 133). Before they dry, insert them onto the tops of the paper clips.

Now you have created an undersea world right in your own house!

NEIGHBORHOOD FUN

Put on a Magic Show

CALLING ALL TRICKSTERS, ACTORS, AND FUN LOVERS!

Has it ever occurred to you that, with a little practice, you too can be a magician? It's true! Oh, sure, in order to saw your assistant in half, or turn a friend into a tiger, you need some pretty fancy equipment. But there are lots of magic tricks that require only the simplest of materials. In fact, it's a lot easier than you think to astound your friends!

SOME MAGIC WORDS:

Abracadabra!

Shazam!

Presto!

Voila!

Bibbity, bobbity, boo!

Alakazam!

Imscray, Amscray!

Itchikaboolah!

Hummena, hummena, hummena!

Whadayaknow!

How 'bout that!

Ipso, facto!

Presto, change-o!

Have a magical time!

BASIC PRINCIPLES OF MAGIC MAKING

THE HAND IS QUICKER THAN THE EYE

A lot of magic is based on this simple truth. What we think we see isn't always what we're really seeing! Take, for instance, the old Shell Game.

There's a coin, or a marble, under one of three shells, or cups. The magician moves the cups around and around, and then asks the audience to pick which shell the coin is under. What makes it so hard is the fact that the magician's hands are quicker than the audience's eyes. Remember, the faster your hands, the more times they'll be wrong. And you can confuse them even more by using another basic law of magic:

MISDIRECTION

Many magic tricks are made possible by the fact that the audience is looking the wrong way at the critical moment. This is no accident, either. Part of a magician's skill is to distract — or misdirect — his audience. If the hidden coin is in your right hand, show them your left hand, and make sure they get a good, long look at it, while the hand with the coin goes unnoticed.

PRACTICE MAKES PERFECT

As easy as the following magic tricks are to do, they still work better the more you practice. Practice in front of a mirror so you can add some of the pizazz that makes magic so much fun!

SECRECY

This may be the oldest and most sacred of all the rules of magic — a magician never tells his tricks! And don't perform the same trick too many times in a row, either. That way your audience won't be able to think too much about how a trick is done.

SOME SIMPLY MAGICAL TRICKS

Mind reading

Your friend picks a number from the face of a watch or clock. You then tell her what number she picked. And you're right — every time!

WHAT YOU'LL NEED:

A watch or clock that has regular numbers on it.

A pencil or pen

HOW TO DO THE TRICK:

Tell your friend to pick any number on the face of the clock. That's any number from one to twelve. He is to keep the number secret from you, although if you want, he can indicate to the rest of the audience which number was chosen. Once he has chosen his number, tell him you are going to start tapping on the face of the clock. Meanwhile, he is to close his eyes, and silently count to twenty, *beginning with the number he has chosen*. He is to count one number for each tap. When he gets to twenty, he is to say "stop!" and open his eyes. Your pencil will be pointing to the number he chose — every time!

HERE'S THE SECRET:

You start tapping with the number eight, and tap backwards, or counterclockwise. Try it and see — it works. This is one of many magic tricks based on the quirks of mathematics.

The power of suggestion

You will make your friend choose the correct pile of cards, without telling her which one to choose!

WHAT YOU'LL NEED:

A deck of regular playing cards
A pencil
A piece of paper

PREPARATION:

Write this message on the paper with your pencil: *"You will choose the 3 pile."* Then, fold up the paper and put it in your pocket.

Take the following cards out of the deck: Ace (1), Two, Three 5s, and four 3s.

Ace
2
Three 5s
Four 3s
Deck face down

With the rest of the deck face down, put the four 3s together, and place them, also face down, on top of the rest of the deck. Put the three 5s together, and place them face down on top of the 3s. Put the 2 face down on top of the 5s, and the ace face down on top of the 2.

Now you're ready to do your trick. Tell your friend that by holding her left hand, you can make her right hand do what you want it to do! She won't believe you, of course, but wait!

Deal out the cards you've prepared, *face down*, in this way:
First pile, the ace and 2.
Second pile, the three 5s.
Third pile, the four 3s.

You should have three piles of cards.

Now put the piece of paper on the table, and grab your friend's left hand. Tell her you're going to try to make her choose a certain pile.

When she touches a pile, you've got her. Here's how:

If she touches the first pile, turn the cards over. Show her that the total of the two cards (Ace (1) and 2), equals *three*. Have your friend read the piece of paper.

If she touches the second pile, spread out the cards in each pile without turning them over. Show her your note, and point out that she chose the only pile with *three* cards in it!

If she touches the third pile, turn over the four 3s, then show her the note. No matter which pile she chooses, you've got her, because she chose the "3" pile!

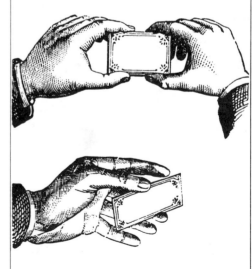

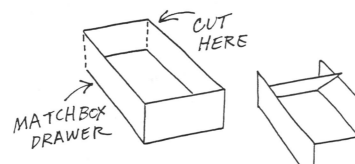

CUT HERE

MATCHBOX DRAWER

ROLLED HANKY

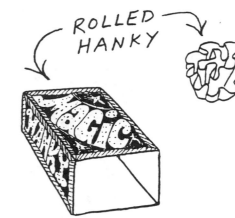

The magical matchbox

You show the audience a large matchbox with the drawer open. They can all see that it is empty. Close the drawer, say the magic word, open it, and with a flourish, pull out a handkerchief!

WHAT YOU'LL NEED:

A large matchbox
(the kind that holds wooden kitchen matches)

Scissors

A small handkerchief

PREPARATION:

Empty the matches out of the box and take out the drawer. Cut two slits down the corners of one end. Roll your hanky into a ball and hide it inside the cover, then put the drawer halfway back in, with the slit end towards the hanky.

HOW TO DO THE TRICK:

Hold the box in your hand, with the back of it toward you, so the hanky is hidden from view. Show the crowd that the box is "empty." Then push the box closed. At the same time, push the hanky with the index finger of your other hand, so the hanky is forced through the slit end into the matchbox. Say the magic word, open the box, and pull out the hanky! Nothing to it!

There are many more simple magic tricks you can do. But if you want to give a longer magic show, just go to your local library and take out some books of magic tricks. Or look in the section of this book called Weird Tricks and Strange Illusions, page 128. Some of these illusions designed to fool yourself will fool your friends just as well!

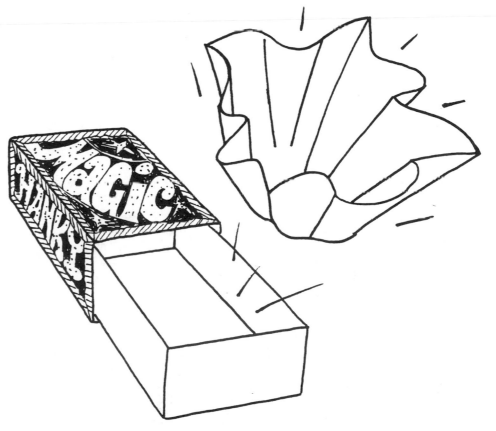

SECRET HELPER TRICKS

Having a secret helper is a great addition to any magic show — and it doubles the fun for you and your helper, too. If you're really a sly magician, you can even have more than one secret helper. But don't tell anyone!

Guess the number of objects

In this trick you will read the mind of your trusty assistant, and correctly guess the chosen object out of the group of ten.

WHAT YOU'LL NEED:

Any ten assorted small objects
(pennies, shells, paper clips, etc.)

Ten numbers written on individual pieces of paper

A secret helper

HOW TO DO THE TRICK:

Line up ten objects on a table. Put numbers in front of them, from one to ten. Leave the room and have someone in the audience point to an object. Then come back in and "read the mind" of your assistant. Have her sit down, and then make a big show of reading her mind. Simply lace your fingertips on her temples, and ask her to close her eyes. When she closes her eyes, you close yours, too. Then murmur, "I must concentrate, con . . . cen . . . trate . . . ."

While you're making a show of your powers of concentration, your assistant will be busy signaling you with the correct answer. How? By clenching her jaw the correct number of times to indicate the chosen object's number. Your fingertips, softly placed on her temples, will easily pick up the number. At last, you announce that you have divined the correct answer. Your friends will be left puzzled and stumped, wracking their brains to figure out how you did it.

Make an object disappear

Even a little kid, as young as four, can be a secret helper for this one.

Take a small object and hold it under a handkerchief or dishtowel. Have the members of your audience feel under the cloth to make absolutely certain that the object is really there. The last person to check however is none other than your secret helper! He feels for it, too, and tells everyone it's there while secretly putting it in his own hand. Now, with a burst of magic words, you pull off the cloth to reveal — nothing! The small object is safely in the hand or pocket of your secret helper, as you proudly receive the amazed oohs and aahs!

Salt and pepper

You can change salt into pepper just by saying the magic word! Well, not really, but your friends will think you did!

WHAT YOU'LL NEED:

A clear salt shaker with a screw-on top

Salt

Pepper

A napkin

PREPARATION:

Make sure there's some salt in the salt shaker. Unscrew the top of the shaker and lay the napkin over the open top. Push the napkin down a bit with your fingertip. Now fill the small depression with pepper. Screw the top back onto the shaker, and tear off the remaining napkin so you can't see any of it.

HOW TO DO THE TRICK:

Pick up the shaker and pour some "salt" into your fist. Say you will change it into pepper. Say the magic word, and open your fist. Presto — pepper!

What's that you say?

If your friend can't hear what you're saying, maybe it's because of that coin in his ear. So reach up and pull it out for him!

WHAT YOU'LL NEED:

A coin. Yes, that's all. Just a coin!

HOW TO DO THE TRICK:

The coin goes between your first and second fingers. It shouldn't show at all from the palm side of your hand.

Ask your friend if he or she would like to "brmphlfmernsml." When he says "What?" you say, "Can't you hear me? Oh. Maybe it's because of this coin in your ear." As you say that, reach up with the hand that's holding the coin. Show your friend only the palm side of your hand as you do this, so he thinks your hand is empty! When your hand is up next to his ear, bend your fingers forward so you can pull the coin into your hand with your thumb.

When you've got it, show your friend the coin you "pulled out of his ear." Tell him he'll hear much better from now on!

Make a magic top hat

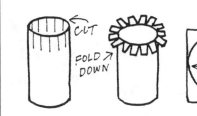
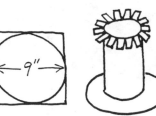

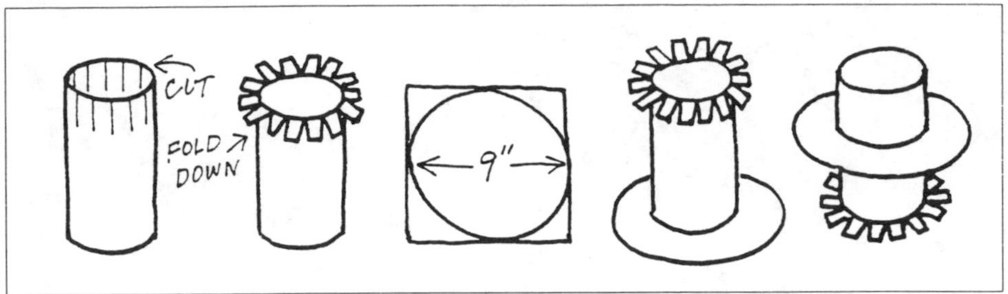

WHAT YOU'LL NEED:

A large empty round oatmeal box (42-oz. [1,100 ml] size is best)

A piece of stiff cardboard

White glue

Scissors

Black poster paint

HOW TO DO IT:

1. Cut 3/4 inch (2 cm) slits all around the open end of your oatmeal box. Make the slits about 1/2 inch (1 cm) apart.
2. Fold out the tabs.
3. Draw a 9 inch (22.5 cm) circle on the stiff cardboard and cut it out. Set the oatmeal box in the center of the circle. Trace around it and cut out the smaller circle. The outer circle is a perfect brim for your hat.
4. Turn the oatmeal box upside down and slip the brim down over the bottom of the box. Glue or tape it to the tabs. If you want, you can make another brim to cover the tabs and strengthen your first brim.
5. Paint the hat black, inside and out.

Too complicated? How about a magic turban instead?

HOW TO DO IT:

Get a 4 1/2 foot (14 m) strip of cotton, in any color. Drape it over your head. Then take the ends, cross them over your head and tuck them in back.

For fun, add a matching sash, and maybe a cape. A magician's costume is an important part of the act! It helps create the mysterious *ambience*, or mood.

Now that you've got a few tricks up your sleeve, and have added a little razzle-dazzle, let's get on with the show!

First, rehearse!

Once you've got everything set, try performing your show alone, just as you're going to do it for your friends. Practice the tricks, what you're going to say before, during, and after each trick, and go through all the motions. Make sure you have everything you'll need. Place your materials (props) just where they need to be for the show, perhaps on a prop table draped with a tablecloth.

• NOW ON WITH YOUR SHOW •

During the show

Some people are more comfortable performing than others. If you're one of them, fine. If not, don't worry. Your tricks, if you've practiced them enough, will speak for themselves. Just relax, and enjoy the magic of the moment!

A few things to remember:
• Take your time!
• When a trick is over, go on to the next one — don't give the audience time to think about how you did it!
• If a trick doesn't work, don't worry — just make a joke about it (you might want to prepare these before the show, just in case), and go on to the next trick.
• Add a lot of mystery and suspense in your preparation. The costume will help. So will a magic wand. But the most important element of mystery is the buildup you give each trick with your words. For instance:

"And now, ladies and gentlemen, a mysterious bit of magic imported from the fabled East! Please try not to gasp in amazement, lest you disturb the cosmic vibrations . . ."

You get the idea . . . .

EXTRA ★★★ EXTRA
READ ALL ABOUT IT!!!

KIDS CAN PUBLISH THEIR OWN NEWSPAPER!

Ever wonder what it's like to be a reporter or an editor? Ever dream of investigating stories and having a *byline* of your very own? Well, stop dreaming and start getting busy. You can publish a neighborhood newspaper over a weekend if you're willing to put in a lot of hard fun — oops, that is, hard work.

Help wanted

Putting a newspaper together is a big job, so you'll need a *staff* to help you. Here are some of the positions you'll need to get the job done.

The *editor or editorial staff* decides exactly what gets in the paper. They can *assign* stories to certain reporters or choose from the stories that reporters bring to them. Editors have the power to fix their reporters' writing, if they need to, or trim a story if it's too long.

Reporters are the backbone of any paper. These are the people who find, and write up, the news. They can work in teams or on their own, investigating the stories they find. If they are writing a *feature*, an important story, they will receive a byline. That means the story will say "by So and So" right after the headline.

Cub reporters are the youngest or most inexperienced staff reporters. If you have some cubs working for your paper, use their abilities as assistant reporters, cartoonists, or artists to draw the pictures in the paper.

The *production staff* are the people who get the paper designed and printed.

The *distribution staff* has the job of getting the paper out to the public.

Of course, people can do more than one job when putting a newspaper out. But it's good to remember which hat you're wearing when, while you're creating your paper. The clearer everyone is about what job he or she is doing, the better your newspaper will be.

THE BIG SCOOP

Now comes the fun. It's time to go around your neighborhood with a pad and pencil to find out what's newsworthy. If you can bring a Polaroid camera with you, so much the better.

Has a new family moved in? Is someone planning a trip? A good reporter always has questions ready. A useful rule of thumb is to ask the *who, what, when, where, why* and *how* about a story.

If you go door to door, you're bound to find more than one story for your paper. You may want to run a feature about someone interesting who lives on your street, even a special pet. As editor, you get to decide which story is the most important. That's called the *lead story*.

When you're writing up your stories, include the who, what, where, why and when in the very first sentence or paragraph.

Here are some sample *headlines* for lead stories:

WHO'S THE FIEND? SOMEONE DRAWS FACE IN O'BRIENS' NEW SIDEWALK!

TOWN TO CUT DOWN MR. FAGAN'S TREE. NEIGHBORS PROTEST

NEW FAMILY AT #33 — WITH FIVE KIDS!

MISSING MAILMAN MYSTERY: NO MAIL TUESDAY

HARLEYS PROMISE BIGGEST BLOCK PARTY EVER

Just the opinions, please

You can also include an opinion poll in your paper. Without naming names, count up how many people are on one side of an issue, and how many on the other. Then publish the results. "Sixty percent of those polled think power mowers are a nuisance on Sunday mornings."

Figuring percentages

An easy way to figure percentages for your newspaper is to ask ten people for their opinion about an issue. Each person then represents 10 percent of the total. For instance, if you ask ten people whether they think cats should be licensed, and seven say yes, and three say no — then 70 percent are in favor of licensing cats and 30 percent are against it.

Don't forget your own opinion

One of the best reasons to put out a paper is to express your own ideas and opinions. That's what an *editorial* is all about. Your editorial can be about anything at all, as long as it's an issue that's important to you and your readers. If your paper has more than one editor, try putting an *op-ed* page together — that's opinions and editorials. You can even include a poem or other style of "think piece" here.

LETTERS, AD COPY, CLASSIFIEDS, AND FILLER

When you tell people about your paper, ask them if they want to contribute a *letter to the editor*. That's a letter written about whatever is on the letter writer's mind!

People may also ask to place an *ad* in your newspaper. If they do, that's great because it will give your newspaper a real professional feeling. A simple way to place an ad is to photocopy someone's business card. If you get enough ads, you can make columns of them, or even a whole page.

The *classified section* is for individuals placing personal ads. These may include lost and found items, or announcements of things for sale.

If you still have room in your paper, use it for *filler*. Filler is anything that might be of interest to your readers, like someone's favorite recipe, gardening tips, or a list of upcoming birthdays of people or pets.

Paste-up and layout

Now that you've got your stories ready, it's time to write them up. Many kids have access to computers with graphics (such as *Print Shop*) and can print their newspaper on it. But let's say for the moment that you don't.

If you're putting out a handwritten edition, **be sure to print clearly.** Give each story a catchy headline, and write up the information in a column 2½" (6 cm) wide. Cut the stories and paste them on a sheet of 11" x 14" (27.5 cm x 35 cm) paper. Any pictures you've taken can be laid in now. Tack them down with a dab of glue.

Your paper will have room for three columns. The lead story will occupy the upper right-hand column.

Make sure you leave room for a *masthead*, too. That's the top line of the newspaper, which tells the paper's name, as well as the date and information about the weather. Many papers also have a *logo*, a special drawing near the masthead.

Sleep tight!

It's time to put your paper to bed — that's what newspaper people say when they're ready to roll the presses. In your case, it means a visit to the nearest copy machine. (If you're not making too many copies, the local shop may print your paper *gratis* — that means free — in exchange for a free ad. No harm in asking, anyway.)

Start spreading the news!

It's time to stop being a journalist, and join the distribution staff as a delivery person. Congratulations! When your paper hits your neighbors' doorsteps, you'll be famous!

MASTHEAD   LOGO
TODAY'S DATE   CHESTER STREET SUN   TODAY'S WEATHER
VOL. 1 - NO. 1

CATCHY HEADLINE MUST GRAB READER

Sun exclusive "Where's my ladder?" Mr. Fagan of number 9 says his ladder has been missing since Saturday. "I swear I hung it up in the garage," Fagan told Sun reporter Alison Sutor. "He probably loaned it to some one", Mrs. Fagan said.

FEATURE OF THE WEEK: AGGIE by Greg Pape
Everyone on State Street knows Aggie. She's lived on the block for over 43 years! But few people know that Aggie was once a sky diver. "It was during World War Two," Aggie told the Sun staff. "My husband Joe was the only
cont'd p. 2

WHO, WHAT, WHERE, WHEN go here. WHY & HOW are next.

BICYCLE RODEO

If you have a bike, you're lucky! Bicycles are one of the best inventions of all time! Not only do they get you where you want to go, but they make you healthy getting there! Riding a bike is great exercise, as well as great fun.

Of course, as with any form of transportation, there are safety rules for bike riding. The number one rule is *always wear a helmet* when you ride. Wearing a helmet will protect you from most serious injuries, in case you fall.

Also, you should *ride where there's little car traffic*, and *follow the general traffic rules*, like stopping on red and going on green. It's also a good idea to *walk across intersections*.

BICYCLE RODEO — THE EVENTS

Slow speed challenge

Try this for something different. Which rider can go the slowest, and still keep his or her balance?

With chalk, mark out three-foot-wide lanes, fifty feet long (that's about half of a football field). Draw thick lines across both ends of the lanes for start and finish lines.

At the call of "Ready, set, ride!" the riders begin going down the course — as slowly as possible. Their feet must remain on the pedals the whole time, though, or they are automatically out.

Last one to reach the finish line is the winner!

The spiral ride

For this test of bicycling skill, you'll need to draw a huge spiral, or two or three. The lanes of the spiral should be about two feet wide (narrower for more experienced riders, wider for beginners). Draw the spiral by beginning in the center and working out. It may help to have two people draw it, using a piece of chalk on a string. One person stays in the center of the spiral, gradually pulling in the string to which the chalk is attached. The other person uses the chalk to draw the spiral. Your spiral should have at least three or four lanes when you're done.

If you only have one spiral, someone should time the riders with the second hand of a watch.

At the call, "Ready, set, ride!" the spiral riders get on their bikes and begin driving to the center, without touching the lines. First one to the center wins.

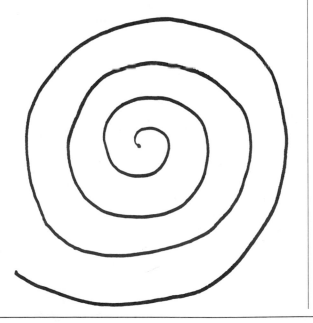

Straight scoot

In this race, riders have to keep inside the lines or they will be ruled out. At a count of "Ready, set, ride!" the race begins. The first person to the finish line wins.

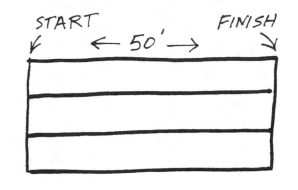

Wavy scoot with balloons

In this more difficult variation of a straight scoot, riders race down a wavy track. At certain intervals, balloons are taped to the ground and the riders must avoid breaking them! As in the straight scoot, they must keep their bike wheels inside the lines, and their feet mustn't touch the ground.

Line lunge

In this difficult test of skill, riders have to keep both their back and front wheels directly on the riding lines. First rider to the finish line wins, but remember, if your wheels go off the lines, you're out! Use the straight scoot track for this contest.

Marble drop

For this contest, you'll need some empty cans, like the ones canned foods come in, and a bunch of marbles. Put the cans on either side of your longest riding track, about fifteen feet apart. The bike rider must ride along the track, dropping a marble into each can as he goes! Think you can do it?

CIRCUS! CIRCUS!

Introducing the fabulous, the amazing, the stupendous, super-talented you! Yes, you can create your very own circus! It takes a bit of planning and a little help from your friends, but the pay-off is well worth the effort. There's magic in a circus — magic you can make yourself!

Getting started

As soon as you've got enough people to put on a show (a minimum of four people), give your circus a name and then start making a few colorful posters to put up for publicity. After all, there can't be a circus without an audience. Be sure the posters include the day, time, and place of performance. Staple the posters around a tree or telephone pole, adding ribbons and balloons for extra effect.

BRING ON THE PERFORMERS!

The abilities and talents of the people in your circus will determine the exact program of acts. Experiment to find the best acts. Here are a few suggestions to get the ball rolling. Once you start rehearsing, you'll find exhibitions of your own to add to the show.

Introducing — the greatest acts the world has ever seen!

RINGMASTER

First of all, no circus can do without the ringmaster. The ringmaster introduces each act, encourages applause, and covers up if things go wrong. Be sure to choose a ringmaster with a loud voice, who likes being the center of attention.

ACROBATS & JUGGLERS

Anyone who can turn a cartwheel, stand on her head, or do a somersault can be a featured performer in your circus. Jugglers are always welcome, too.

CLOWNS

Send in the clowns — the more the merrier! Everybody loves a clown. But remember, clowning around is serious business. Each clown needs to have a unique personality and a special act to express it through. A clown can be happy, sad, clumsy, confident, or silly, but he must always be true to himself.

Experiment to find out which kind of clown is inside you, just waiting to come out. Give your clown a name. Then ask yourself, how does your clown act when she's feeling sad? Happy? Angry? Brave? Ask a friend to interview you as a clown. You can't answer any questions in words, though. You'll have to communicate with your face and body movements. Keep in mind that clowns are not ordinary, everyday people. Every little motion they make has to be big and exaggerated. Move around being a clown. Try a few different funny walks until you find one that feels right for you. Then stick with it whenever you're clowning.

THE ACTS!

Hand stands, somersaults, cartwheels, and juggling are traditional circus feats. The key to pulling them off in a backyard circus is to perform each trick with *pizazz*. Before and after each feat, the performer should face the audience, hands held proudly overhead. After the applause, the performer skips off quickly while the ringmaster blows the whistle for the next act.

BROOMSTICK BALANCING

How about an act that allows a performer to defy gravity — right in front of the audience's astonished eyes? It's Broomstick Balancing.

Here's how it's done. Place a broomstick in the palm of your outstretched hand. Your goal is to keep it standing as long as possible. (During the performance, the seconds can be pounded out on the bottom of a pot with a wooden stick or rubber mallet. Or, the ringmaster can build excitement by leading the audience in a count.)

Secrets of broomstick balancing

1. Keep your eyes glued to the top of the stick.
2. When the stick starts to fall, either step in the direction it's falling or reach your arm that way. Don't do both at once, though, or the stick will surely fall.
3. If the stick is falling, lowering your hand may help; raising it never will.

With a little practice, you'll be surprised at how long you can keep the stick up — and your audience will be totally amazed!

THE CLOWN SHOW

A clown show is a special act in the circus that features clowns. These shows-within-the-show should be interspersed with other circus acts.

Make sure each clown has a chance to say hello to the audience during the clown show. Since clowns don't talk, they say hello by waving, or tipping their hat when they first see the audience. A funny way to say hello is to walk into the performance arena pretending that you don't see the audience at first. When you see them, act surprised.

Here are a few ideas for clown shows to get you started:

MAKE A WIND-UP CLOWN

Cut a large key from heavy cardboard, color it grey, and then tape or sew it onto the clown's back. The ringmaster pretends to wind the key up to get the clown going. But soon, the clown winds down, moving slower and slower until it flops over like a rag doll. The ringmaster then gives the key another turn and points the clown to the exit.

THE BARBER ACT

One clown plays the barber, the other plays the customer. The barber holds a giant-sized comb and scissors, cut from cardboard. The customer clown comes into the arena and sits. Distressed, he points to his hair. The barber clown starts "cutting," with much gusto and flailing elbows. When he's finished, the barber hands the customer a hollow cardboard "mirror." The customer is not pleased. Without speaking, the two argue until the customer angrily chases the barber out of the ring!

MORE STUPENDOUS ACTS ••

IRON MAN, OR WOMAN OF STEEL

This time-tested act can be performed with sheer acting ability. To make big muscles, roll socks around both upper arms and tape them so they stay up. Then put on a form fitting, long sleeved shirt. Voila! Bulging biceps!

The weight is made from black balloons taped to both ends of a broomstick. Paint a big white number on the balloons — say 2000 lbs.

The ringmaster introduces the strong person who strides on, proudly flexing his muscles. The weight is then carried on by as many people as possible. Grunting, they lay it at the feet of the strong person, who picks it up, very, very slowly. The more horribly he suffers, the better. Gritting his teeth in agony, he transfers the weight to one hand, and raises it high. Then the ringmaster calls for applause, as the strong person slowly lowers the weight, panting from exertion. After his bow, he faints and is helped off by the assistants.

And don't forget . . . .

THE TWO-HEADED WOMAN

For this act you'll need a large, long dress or bathrobe. Two girls stand side-by-side with their inside arms around each other's waist. Their inside legs are tied together. Put the dress on them with their outside arms in the sleeves. Drape a scarf around their necks to hide their shoulders; add a belt around the waist.

When the ringmaster introduces them, he or she asks how they want to entertain the audience. Head One says she wants to sing, but Head Two says she can't bear One's singing. Two suggests telling jokes, but One blows all the punchlines. The ringmaster suggests they come back later. Miffed, they decide to leave. One turns her head left, and Two turns hers right. Finally they manage to walk off in the same direction.

Another sure-fire showstopper . . . .

WILD ANIMAL ACT

If you don't happen to have any Bengal tigers or dancing bears roaming your neighborhood, and if the local pets are more lovable than ferocious, don't worry. Lots of kids, especially little ones, love to act like wild animals. They can use their natural acting ability to snarl, growl, and snap at the animal trainer. After the crack of the trainer's whip, however, the fearsome beasts turn into lovable kittens, purring happily. They stride off obediently when the trainer asks them to.

And how about . . . .

★ ★ ★ ★ ★ ★ ★ ★ ★

Ten Ways to Say Terrific

amazing
★
astounding
★
marvelous
★
fabulous
★
stupendous
★
miraculous
★
wondrous
★
extraordinary
★
mind-boggling
★
staggering

★ ★ ★ ★ ★ ★ ★ ★ ★

Strike up the band!

If you have authentic circus music available, great. But if not, Tchaikovsky's *Nutcracker Suite* can be used effectively. If not, how about some of John Philip Sousa's marches?

Drumrolls are a great addition to any circus. So are cymbals clashing at the proper moments. If you don't have cymbals, the lids of pots will do. At the very least, be sure to have noise makers on hand.

Raising the big top

A backyard is the perfect place for a circus. Start by decorating the backyard with ribbons and balloons, as you set up the chairs or blankets for the audience to sit on. You can mark a semicircle in the grass with a piece of rope or a thin line of sprinkled baby powder. That will define the performance area.

On the day of the performance, you'll need two identical lists of the acts in the order that they'll be performed. One list is for the ringmaster. The other will be posted where the performers can see it during the performance.

GLITZ AND SPARKLE — PUTTING ON MAKEUP

When it comes to circuses, the more glitz and sparkle, the better. Bright red lips and cheeks, colorful eye shadows and eye liners will make the performers really stand out. Be sure to leave making up for last, though, so your makeup will be bright and fresh for the performance. A good time to apply makeup is about forty-five minutes before the show begins.

Clown face

Making up in clown face is an art. White greasepaint makeup is best for the background of the face, but if there's none on hand, try a thin coat of cold cream dusted with cornstarch powder. Be sure to cover your hair with a hat or shower cap before you start working.

Start your makeup by applying white over your entire face. (It's not necessary to put it on the neck or ears.) When you're finished, dust your face with white powder, then brush any excess away with a soft makeup brush. Next, fill in any red places, like the cheeks, lips, the tip of the nose, or markings on the side of the eyes. Dust these with powder as before. Finally, add any black markings. For example, you might want to make triangles for eyebrows, or dot several freckles on your cheeks. Have fun designing your clown face, but remember to keep it simple.

Remove the makeup with baby oil and soft tissues.

AND NOW . . . LET THE SHOW BEGIN!

Play recorded music on a portable tape player as the audience files in. When everyone is ready, stop the music. The ringmaster steps forward and says, *"Ladies and gentlemen, and children of all ages, welcome to the fabulous, the amazing — Street Circus!"* At this signal, the music comes on again as the performers all parade in front of the audience, waving and smiling. When they finish, the ringmaster blows his whistle and announces the first act.

Now you can add a dash of extra-special something . . . .

Razzle dazzle!

By now, you've probably gotten the message. Where circuses are concerned, a dash of flash is good — but a truckload is even better! Circus time is not the time for truth or modesty, so don't be afraid to lay it on thick!

The ringmaster introduces each act as if the performers were world famous *artistes*, just arrived from an exotic land.

At the end of each act, the ringmaster should brazenly call for applause.

The grande finale

End your circus with another parade, this time led by the ringmaster. Be sure to show off as much as you can, as you wave and blow kisses to your adoring audience! Then, the performers all join hands for one last bow. Ta-da!

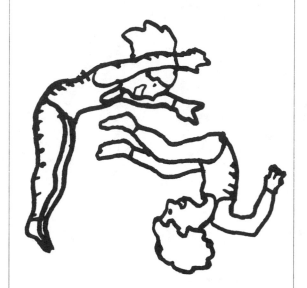

CRAFTING COSTUMES

Reach deep into your box of dress-up clothes, costumes, and old clothes and jewelry. Add some cardboard, scissors, glue, sparkles, feathers, and paint. Bring along plenty of imagination and go wild! Making costumes is one of the best parts of putting on a circus . . . second only to wearing them in the arena!

RINGMASTER

The ringmaster will need a top hat, (see Magic Show, p. 112), high boots, a colorful sash, and a sweater or jacket to which "tails" have been attached. He or she carries a cane or stick and a whistle.

ACROBATS

Girls wear tights with flouncy short skirts and sparkling headbands. Boys wear their shirts open at the neck and colorful bandanas.

CLOWNS

Put a clown costume together by searching for old clothes — the bigger, the better. Suspenders, vests, hats, and ties add to the fun, especially when their colors don't match. For clown shoes, try a pair of a big man's shoes. Another way to create oversized shoes is to glue foam rubber to a pair of old sneakers, and spray paint the whole construction.

WILD ANIMALS

Kids performing as wild animals can wear animal-colored jogging suits with shredded rope tails pinned on. Mop-head wigs, or hairbands to which yarn hair and cardboard ears have been attached add to the effect.

GARAGE $ALE

Are the knick-knacks on the mantlepiece piled three high? Do you have to wade through the sea of boxes in your attic to get to the box you want? Is your basement stacked to the ceiling with dust-covered treasures?

If you answered "Yes" to any of these questions, *wake up*! This weekend may be the perfect time for a *Family Garage Sale*.

GET ORGANIZED

First, clear a large area for sorting out the wheat from the chaff, the treasure from the trash, the gold from the fool's gold — you get the point. You'll probably need a whole room, like the living room or dining room.

Have some large garbage bags on hand. Also a couple of cartons for giveaways.

Giveaways

Many churches, charities, and organizations are grateful for donations of used clothing and housewares. Some have drop-off places in supermarket parking lots for clean giveaway items. If there's no drop-off place where you shop, call a local church or synagogue. Salvation Army and Volunteers for America are two large organizations that may take your giveaways.

If you would like to have a more personal relationship with the people you're giving to, there's an organization called *The Box Project* that your family can join. It will match your family with a family that can use the kinds of things you need to clear out every so often. There's a small fee to join and sending the boxes does cost money. But it's fun to know who'll be getting your old stuff. They'll write to you, and when you send a box, you write to them. Many people in The Box Project become faraway friends with the families they mail to. For more information send a postcard to: The Box Project, PO #435, Plainville, CT 06062-0435.

Pricing

Once you've sorted out the giveaway stuff, it's time to look over the things you want to sell. The next big question is: "What to charge for all these choice tidbits?"

Actually, pricing is half the fun, even if it is agony. It's a guessing game — you've got to guess what the item will be worth to *somebody* else.

Publicity

In order to sell, you're going to need customers. If you live on a well-traveled road, you're lucky. Just put out a large sign, and tie ribbons around the trees in the front of your house.

If you live on a side street, try parking a car at the corner, with a large sign in the back window pointing in the direction of your house.

Some local newspapers don't charge much for garage

sale notices, either, so you can take out an ad in the paper. And your neighborhood store might let you hang a poster announcing your sale, if you promise to take it down as soon as the sale is over.

Where to have the sale

Naturally, the garage is a perfect place. That way, you don't have strangers barging through your house. And if it rains, your stuff doesn't get wet.

Another name for garage sale is "yard sale." If you've got a yard, and it's going to be good weather, it's nice to put everything out where you can sit in the sun and enjoy the day. A good idea might be to start out with your stuff in the garage, then move some of it out if the weather looks good.

If you live in the city, you might be able to use the stoop of your building, if you get permission. Or, try the sidewalk near your house. Some city dwellers put up notices for an "apartment sale," and hold the sale right in their apartments.

SETTING UP

YOU'LL NEED:

Tags or stickers
Pens and markers
Tables or blankets to put things on
A cash box such as a shoe box

When you've decided on prices, mark each item by putting a sticker on it.

Bargaining

When you put a price on an item, realize that you might have to sell it for less. If after half an hour or so, items are getting bought like crazy, and nobody's trying to talk the price down, you've probably priced the items too low. On the other hand, if people are just coming to look or are even asking you if you'll take less for items, you've probably priced your stuff too high.

If you're in the right price range, people will come up to you and say, "What's your best price on this?" or "Will you take such and such amount for this?" At that point, it's up to you to decide. You might decide in advance to take, say, 20 percent less on any item than the price tag says. But a better idea is to play it by ear. The key is *knowing your market*. That means getting a sense of what something is worth.

The Aftermath

Well! Take a deep breath and let out a cheer. You've sold a lot of stuff, hopefully, and you've learned a lot about business (and about human behavior!). You've also cleared up a lot of the clutter that had been clogging up your house. Now you've got room and money to buy new things and make new clutter!

GOOD TIMES AT HOME
Family Fairy Tale

Forsooth! As you well know, your family's story is the stuff of legend. Well, why not turn it into one?

Making up a family fairy tale is easier than it sounds, actually. And a lot of fun, besides. There are basically two ways to go about lionizing your family:

1. Build on an existing fairy tale

2. Make up one from scratch

Just a note on terms: We'll call the story a fairy tale from here on in, for simplicity's sake. It may be more of a myth, or legend, or fable, or epic, or saga, or whatever!

USING AN EXISTING FAIRY TALE

Think of your favorite classic tale. You probably have several. Examine them, thinking about which set of characters sounds the most like the members of your family. Are you like *The Three Bears* — with just mom, dad, and you? Or like *Hansel and Gretel*, with a brother or sister? Do you fit well as animals — say, the characters in the *Winnie The Pooh* books or *Wind in the Willows*? Or with fantastical characters, like those in *Alice in Wonderland*?

By now, your mind is probably coming up with ideas by the dozens! You can use the characters in the story to represent each of your family members. Like this: "Papa Bear Smith and Mama Bear Smith had a little boy bear named Johnny . . . ." But you don't have to use the events of the story. You can make up your own events.

STARTING FROM SCRATCH

So you're feeling brave, you stout yeomen, you! Okay, how about making up your family fairy tale from scratch? It's a blast! Is your dad a king or a sultan, or is he more like The Little Peasant? Is your sister the clever serving girl or a princess? Is your brother a friendly bear or a noble knight?

If you are making up your own story, you have to know what it's about first. Is it the story of how you all came to be a family? Of how you came to live in this house together? Of how you found your household pet? You should be able to say what it is in one fairly short sentence . . . ." This is a story about the day the wind blew the roof off." That way, you'll stay clear about it while you're writing, and your story will be neat and to the point.

Language

Part of the fun of making a family fairy tale is in the words you use. Try to keep your fairy tale in fairy tale language — use lots of antique words and fancy turns of phrase. Like this: "Long ago, in ye olde days before Sir Telly invented Tellyvision . . . ."

Making the book

You'll want to include lots of funny drawings, or beautiful ones, if someone in the family is a regular Rembrandt. And some fancy calligraphy is nice, too, if you're ambitious.

For more about making the actual book, see *The Book of Me*, page 36.

FAMILY COAT OF ARMS

Does your family have its own coat of arms? You might be surprised to find out that yours does. (There is a Heraldic Register you can consult to find out.)

But for the rest of us, whose families were never noble, *now's our chance!* We can design our own coat of arms, with our own family motto.

What would be your *family animal?* An eagle? A bear? A chicken? Think hard — once you've chosen an animal, your whole family is stuck with it forever (or at least until you design a new coat of arms!).

What would your *family symbol* be? A flag? A rose? A sword? A basket of fruit? A tree? Try to make a design using your family animal and your family symbol. An eagle holding a sword, for example. Or, a chicken standing by a basket of fruit, pecking away.

Now draw a shield around the picture. All coats of arms are displayed on shields (when they're not on flags, that is).

WEIRD TRICKS AND STRANGE ILLUSIONS

Hot or cold?

Set out three pots of water — one as hot as you can comfortably stand, one with a tray of ice cubes in it, and the one in the middle at room temperature. Stick one hand in the hot water, the other in the cold water. Then put both hands in the middle pot. It will feel hot to one hand, cold to the other! Is the water hot or cold? It just goes to show you, everything's relative!

Wet or dry?

Put on a rubber glove and stick your hand into a pot of cold water. Your hand will feel wet, even though it's really dry. Now put the same hand in hot water — it won't feel nearly as wet! That's because our sense of touch judges wetness partly by how cold it is.

Make a fool of yourself

Can you sign your name? Oh, yeah? Try to write your name on a piece of paper while at the same time you trace a circle on the floor with your foot. Bet you can't!

Make the earth move

Put your forehead on the handle of a baseball bat and the head of the bat on the floor. Circle the bat three times in this position, and stand up — earthquake! ! !

Name that food

Put a blindfold on a friend, and some nose clips, too. Let her taste an apple, a raw potato, and a slice of raw onion. Ask her to tell you the difference! It won't be easy, that's for sure, and you know why! That's right, our sense of taste depends on our sense of smell. No wonder nothing tastes good when we have colds.

Sound effects

We've all heard the sound of the sea when putting our ear to a seashell. But how about —

Fire: Crumple a large piece of cellophane.
Thunder: Shake a flexible cookie sheet.
Foghorn: Blow across a soda bottle.
Gunshot: Whack a ruler on wood or leather.
Machine gun: Two pencils drumming on the bottom of an empty box.
Explosion: Blow up a paper bag and pop it.
Train: Rub two sanding blocks together.
Voice on phone: Talk into a plastic cup.
Footsteps in snow: Strike a bag of flour on a hard surface.

Add some sound effects of your own. It works especially well if you have a microphone or if you can make a tape. Record a story with sound effects, to entertain your friends and family. The more sound effects you use, the better it'll be!

Rubber pencil

Hold the end of a pencil between your thumb and forefinger. Shake your hand up and down quickly. Whoa! Is that pencil wobbly or what?

Hole in your hand

Get a tube of paper   the inside of a paper towel roll or toilet tissue roll is perfect — and put the tube to your eye. Now focus both eyes on a distant object, at least 15 feet (5 m) away. Got it? Okay, now bring your hand in front of the eye that is not looking through the tube. Move your hand back and forth, in the way and out of the way, until you see the hole in your hand. Don't be scared — it's not really there, of course.

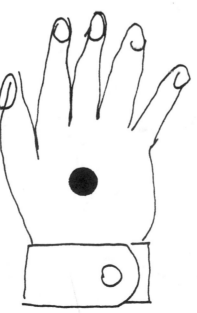

OPTICAL ILLUSIONS

A. Which corner is nearest to you?
B. Is this book opening toward you or away from you?
C. Where is the middle leg attached?
D. Which is bigger? (They're both the same!)
E. Which is longer? (They're both the same!)

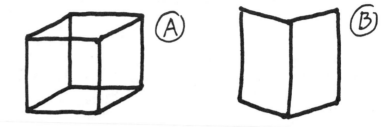

DESIGN A MODEL CITY

How many toys do you have lying around the house? Make that, how many hundreds of toys? If you're like most kids (and some adults, too), you've probably collected a number of playthings over the years. You may have stuffed animals, model cars, planes, wood and plastic building blocks, dolls, dollhouses, dinosaurs, and perhaps a set of trains from a holiday gone by.

Well, don't worry. There's a way your seldom used toys can get a second chance in life. A weekend is the perfect time to trot them all out and put them to work building a city!

The only thing you'll have to forget about is the difference in sizes between your various toys. For the purposes of your model city, they'll all have to get along and work together.

Inside or out?

This activity is ideal if you have an attic or a basement space that's out of the way of normal household traffic. Once you've put in the work of building your city, you'll probably want to leave it set up for a while. On the other hand, if it's a beautiful day, you may want to work outside in a sandbox, on the lawn, under a tree, or on some asphalt (where you can draw in roads with chalk).

Start with the roadwork

Blocks strung out in long lines make fine roads for a model city. Also, be alert for any large pieces of cardboard or poster board that may come your way. You can paint roads and parks on them very easily with poster paint. If your parents are willing to donate a worn out sheet, you can use it to paint roads on as well. You might paint them with fabric paint, if you want to keep the ground work for another day. Paint the sheet the night before you begin building your model city.

Your city will need a super highway as well as some smaller, curvy streets in the residential section. Use green paint to fill in parks and lawns.

A planned community

Just like the real thing, your model city will be a place where creatures live and work together. Consider making an industrial area on the outskirts of town. Toy construction trucks and cranes can help get the job done here. Building the city is as much fun as sending your play people and dolls there to live after the city is completed.

Use blocks to create large buildings and warehouses in the industrial area. Make sure your roadwork enables the creatures of your town to get to work, too.

You'll need to make stores, too, so the townspeople can get the things they need. And housing, of course, so the people who live in your city have a place to live and relax. If you don't have enough blocks to make houses for all of your town citizens, make more from empty paper milk containers, or upside down shoe boxes.

Milk carton skyscrapers

Milk containers make good apartment houses, office buildings, and houses of worship in a model city. Glue construction paper to them. Don't try to paint the cartons if they have waxy surfaces.

Shoe box houses

Take the lid off the box and turn the box upside down. Cut along three sides of the top (used to be the bottom) of the box to make a hinged roof. This will allow you to place people in and take them out of the house.

Cut out windows and a door. For fancy windows, tape a piece of clear cellophane, like the kind that comes on pasta boxes, on the inside of the cut out window.

Color or paint the house with a brick or stone design, or as you wish. Color or paint the lid to look like the outside. Cut small bushes from green paper and paste them on.

You can add to the effect of your shoe box house by making a peaked roof for it. Cut both short end flaps of the lid off. Fold the lid lengthwise and set it on top of the house.

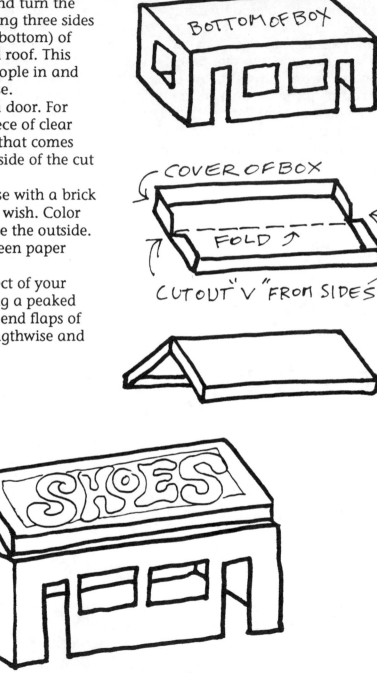

Getting around town

Arrange any cars in fleets. If you have enough, you can have a car dealership in town. Put parking lots in back of the stores or around your mall, if your town has one.

Designate a place for an airport, too. But remember to put it on the outskirts of town, where airport noise won't be too bothersome.

Do most of your town creatures need cars? Better provide them with driveways.

How about a public works department where trucks can be parked? Or a bus terminal for city and school buses? And don't forget emergency vehicles.

PLAY CLAY RECIPE

1 1/2	cups (375 ml) flour
1/2	cup (125 ml) salt
1/2	cup (125 ml) water
1/4	cup (50 ml) vegetable oil
Food coloring	

Mix the flour and salt. Slowly add the oil, water and coloring. Knead the clay by pulling and pushing it. If it's sticky, add more flour. Store in the refrigerator, in an air-tight plastic container.

(If you create something you want to keep, bake the clay for 2 hours in a 250°F (120°C) oven. When it's cooled, "paint" it with white glue. When the glue dries, the creation can be colored with markers or waterpaints.)

Landscaping

You can make trees for your model city by collecting small sticks and twigs, and glueing on crushed green tissue paper. Make a base for the trees from clay or homemade salt dough.

You can make gardens and trees from cut-out pictures from magazines, too. Glue them onto cardboard, cut them out, and add a back so they will stand.

More ideas for your model city

A theme park zoo for jungle creatures, a lake or swimming pool in a bowl or basin for waterproof creatures, a parade down Main Street, a "rush hour" when the work day is over, police and fire departments, a locomotive around the town. Let your imagination come up with more ideas for your model city! As they say, "The sky's the limit". . . or is it?

CUT OUT PICTURE OF A TREE + GLUE TO CARDBOARD

TAPE OR GLUE TO FOLDED CARDBOARD

CRUSHED GREEN TISSUE PAPER

TWIG

CLAY OR SALT DOUGH

Calling all time travelers! It's time to stake a claim in the future while you take a place in history! You can do it by burying a time capsule that you created yourself.

What's a time capsule? It's a container filled with mementos and information about you, and the time you live in. It gets planted in the earth so that someone in the future will come along, open it, and know about the life you live. The very first one was created in ancient Babylonia by some clever person who put a few odds and ends into the cornerstone of a building he was working on. Thousands of years later, when the building was excavated by archaeologists, those odds and ends — or *artifacts* — were discovered. From them, scientists learned about everyday life in a long ago time.

Today, people are still making time capsules so they can communicate with people of the future.

PREPARING THE CAPSULE

In order to have a time capsule that will withstand time and weather, be on the lookout for a plastic container that can be sealed very tightly. Test the container by pouring water inside it, drying it off, and turning it upside down. No water should leak out.

When you've found the right container, place the contents you want to bury inside. For additional protection, wrap the lid with wide postal tape. Packed carefully, your capsule and its contents should last at least an *eon* — and that's a very long time!

What goes in, will come out

Choosing what to put inside your time capsule is up to you, of course, as long as you limit your choices to things small enough to fit in your container.

Think about small objects that you have around the house. A baseball card, a paper clip, some pennies, a ball point pen, the headline cut out of a newspaper. . . . These ordinary objects may seem mundane to you, but imagine how someone who lives far in the future might view them. Three thousand years from now, a paper clip will be a fascinating clue for a historian.

A LETTER TO THE FUTURE

Why not write a personal message to the finder of your capsule? A letter is a good way to do this. Be sure to write down the date, especially the year, that you made your message.

Tell about your everyday life. Where do you get food? What tools do you use, and for what jobs? What games do you play? What are the main energy sources in your life? How do you get from place to place?

Find pictures in a used magazine to show the finder of your capsule what the things you wrote about look like. Cut out pictures of buildings that seem typical or anything else that shows the way we live today.

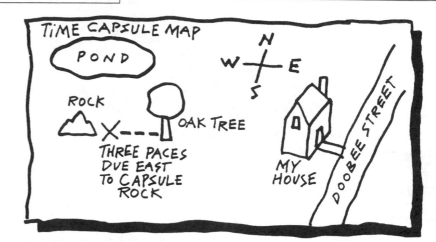

Burying the capsule

Once you've assembled the contents of your capsule, it's time to bury it. The capsule should be buried at least six inches deep and marked carefully.

A large boulder makes a good marker. If you have a chisel and hammer, carve out the words *Time Capsule* or perhaps the year on the face of the rock. You can use waterproof paint to mark your capsule, too, even nail polish. But you'll have to give it an extra coat in a year or two.

Measure the location of the capsule from the nearest tree, too, and write this information down in a few separate places. Keep one for yourself. Give a couple to other people. If your family has a safe deposit box, ask if you can put in an index card that tells where the capsule is.

Careful you don't lose it!

The biggest problem with time capsules is remembering where they have been buried! Portland, Oregon, and Phoenix, Arizona are just two of the cities that have lost track of their official city time capsules! The town of Corolla, California has even offered a $100 reward to anyone who can find just one of its many lost capsules!

You'll be part of history

When you create a time capsule, you are opening a window onto the future, and giving those who come after a chance to look in on the past. It's a good feeling to be part of history!

WIDE, WIDE WORLD

A Day at the Beach

Ah, the smell of fresh salt air with a cool sea breeze blowing through your hair! Sand dunes for climbing, castles to create, shells to find, exotic sea creatures to visit in their tidal pool homes . . . .

It's all at the beach — only at the beach! So whether you're a half a day's journey or a stone's throw away, get your gear together and come on! The weekend is a perfect time to enjoy and explore the beach.

What to bring

Of course, you'll bring your family, friends, and bathing suit. You won't forget sunglasses, towel, a crazy beach hat, pails, and things to dig with, either. And don't leave out *sunscreen*! Use it freely, from the tips of your ears to the tops of your feet. The sun can be strong at the beach, and sunburn is no fun.

Carry an extra big T-shirt, and a sweatshirt, too. A T-shirt is good to wear when you're exploring the shore. And you'll be happy to have the sweatshirt, if a warm ocean breeze suddenly turns chilly.

Don't forget beach shoes, either — they're important on a seaside exploration. Broken shells are sharp to step on, and a rocky shore can be slippery. Any shoes that have rubber soles and can get wet — like a pair of old sneakers — will do fine.

For beachcombing, bring a few plastic or *mesh bags*. A *sieve* is a good idea, for sifting sand. A *net* is useful, too, if you want to look at a few sea creatures more closely for a short time. As long as you return them to their watery home, they won't mind spending a brief time with you. To make a net, see page 139.

BATHING SUIT

SUNGLASSES

TOWEL

BEACH HAT

PAIL & SHOVEL

SUNSCREEN

SWEAT SHIRT

BEACH SHOES

NET

High tide, low tide

High tide is when the level of the ocean rises; low tide is when it falls. Tides are caused by the pull of the moon's gravity, tugging at the water here on Earth. The sea changes from high tide to low tide twice a day.

The best beachcombing happens right after the tide goes out, during low tide. That's when you'll find all the treasure the high tide left behind. Check a seaside newspaper for the time of the tides. Look on the weather page. Then plan your trip to include low tide.

SAND IS SENSATIONAL

When you wiggle your toes in sand, you are wiggling them in ancient history! Long, long ago, the action of water and wind broke up mountains, rocks, shells, and coral, to make sand. A rock from a mountaintop forest may have tumbled down a river and out to sea. There it would have been ground into sand by the pounding surf. How long did the journey take from top of the mountain to speck in the sea? Hundreds, thousands, maybe millions of years!

If you bring a small container or spice bottle to the beach, you can collect some sand in it. It's fun to collect a bottle from every beach you visit. The sand inside each of them will be different!

Sand patterns

Stand with your back to the ocean and look up at the beach. What patterns do you see? Do you see wind patterns where the wind blew over the sand? Do you see tracks of birds or hermit crabs? Can you tell where the water was at high tide? The sand will tell you many things, if you take the time to read it.

A SEASHORE ZOO

As long as you return them before you go home, it's okay to collect sea creatures you see at the beach. You can house them in a pail, or even better, in a see-through container, where you can watch their antics.

Before you go looking for creatures, though, prepare a salt water habitat, so they can spend their time with you in comfort. Put some sand, a few rocks, and some seaweed in your container, and then add the seawater. Make sure the water doesn't get too hot in the sun. Your sea creature friends will feel right at home in the habitat you've made for them.

IS ANYBODY HOME?

No matter how deserted a beach may look, there's wildlife to be found in the sand. (And watch out! A few of the creatures who make their homes there, like sandflies, bite!)

Most sand creatures, however, are peaceable. Many are shy, too, living under the sand as they do. If you press your ear to the sand and listen carefully, you may hear them digging and building.

Seaworms make burrows in the sand. Look for holes that they've made or for birds pecking at the sand to find them. Some of these strange creatures build themselves hard tunnels by making the sand into cement! An empty seaworm shell is a real treasure to find at the beach.

Use your sieve to shake out some sand and find the creatures living in it. If you don't find anything, go deeper. They're down there, you can be sure of that!

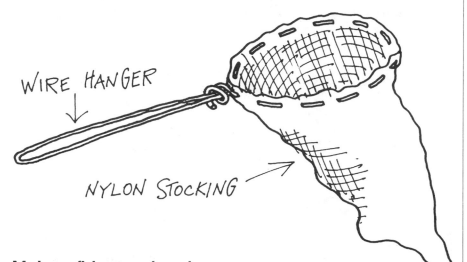

WIRE HANGER

NYLON STOCKING

Make a fisherman's net

To collect the creatures you'll later return to the wild, you can make a net from a woman's nylon stocking. With pliers, form a wire hanger into the shape of a question mark. Using the top end as if it were a needle, push the ankle part of the stocking through until it is attached all the way around. Then close the top of the question mark, by attaching it to the other part of the hanger.

Peek-a-boo!

The first thing to know about a shell is if it's dead and empty, or alive and occupied! Naturally, the answer will make an enormous difference in what you do next!

If you suspect someone's living in a shell you've found, examine it carefully. Try to peek inside, but never stick anything into the shell to prompt a response. If the inhabitant inside feels safe and comfortable, it may come out and look around.

You can put your mollusk friend in the temporary habitat you've created. If you added enough sand, you will see him snuggle down into it. He may open up to take a look at you with a periscope eye. Remember to put him back in the exact spot where you first found him, before the water in your bucket gets warm.

Hello, Molly!

Empty shells that you find on the beach are actually skeletons of boneless animals called *invertebrates*. The shell is formed from special fluid the mollusk produces that hardens as the animal grows.

Some mollusks, called *univalves* or snails, have one shell only. It is made when the animal coils and twirls around as it grows. The kind of shell you can put your ear to, to hear the whole ocean, is a univalve. (Of course, it's not the ocean's roar you're really hearing. It's actually the same sound that's around you all the time. The shape of the shell has just amplified it. Your ear is coiled in a similar way to make hearing easier.)

Other mollusks, called *bivalves*, come with two shells. Clams, oysters, and mussels are common bivalves. The two shells are held together by a piece of muscle. But when the shell is washed up on shore, the attachment has usually broken. That's why you often find only half of a bivalve.

Talented shells

No, they can't sing — but some can dance! Many shell inhabitants have what's called a *foot*, that they use for traveling. With their foot, they can slide, hop, and jump. Some scallop shells zig-zag through the water. The scallops open their shells to take water in, then squeeze it out to propel them along — nature's jet propulsion.

Shells have all sorts of talents. Take the *Chinese Hat*, for example. It can resist the prying fingers of an adult, even though the tiny creature is just one inch long.

The *Abalone* has healing powers. Abalone juice helps people to fight infection and viruses. The state of California has a law to protect Abalones.

HER MAJESTY, THE MUREX BRANDARIS

Long ago, back before 1600 *B.C.*, a shell was found which secreted a dye that made material yellow, green, blue, red or purple — depending on how long the clothes were steeped in it. The red and purple were brilliant, rich shades, unlike any other that people had known. Eight thousand shells were crushed and boiled to make just one gram of precious color.

The Indians of Central America and Mexico still use the beautiful Murex dye. But they are much smarter than their ancient counterparts. They gently squeeze a drop of dye from each shell and then return it to its home in the ocean. That way, there will always be a good supply of shells and colors!

The *Collector Mollusk*

Some mollusks use their shells for recycling, too. The Collector Mollusk travels at night, looking for bits of rock and coral to glue onto his own shell. Once the shells are secure, the Collector travels on, now better camouflaged, thanks to the reused "junk" on his back!

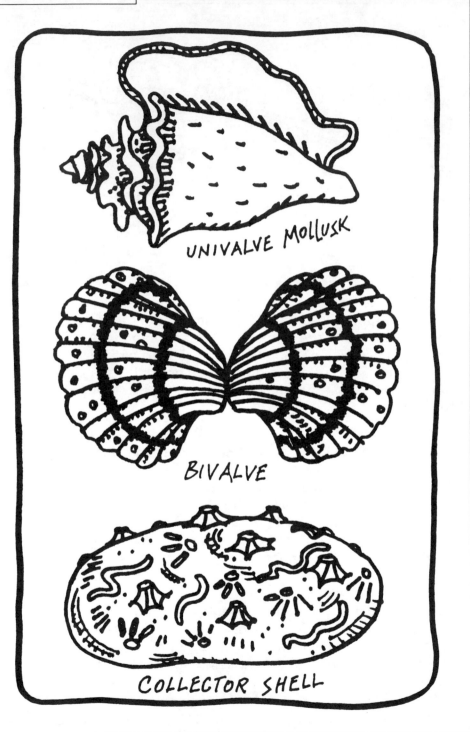

UNIVALVE MOLLUSK

BIVALVE

COLLECTOR SHELL

SEEK OUT SEAWEED

Seaweeds — also called algae — are amazing plants that live in the ocean. They come in three colors: green, brown and red. The green ones live close to the water's edge; the brown ones come from further out, and the reds live in the ocean depths. They don't have leaves or stems like garden plants, because they get all the food they need from sea water passing over them.

Look for seaweed in rocky places along the shore. Often you will find little creatures in it, if you sift through the algae.

Pressed seaweed

With their feathery shapes, and delicate branches, algae are pleasing to look at on paper. They seem to float there, just the way they did in their watery home. (You can make a beautiful tray for someone special using algae, too. See Classy Gifts To Make, page 156.)

To press seaweed, right at the ocean's edge, bring along a flat pan (like a cake pan), a piece of heavy paper, and some newspaper.

If you want to press it at home, transport the algae in a small amount of sea water, carried in a strong plastic bag that's been tied really tightly. (Ask a grown-up to make sure it's leakproof.)

Fill the cake pan with salt water and place the algae in. The plant will spread out, floating on the water. Use a toothpick or fingertip to arrange the seaweed into a shape you like.

Then, gently slide the paper under the plant, and lift it out, holding both sides. (A friend can help here.) Let the water drain off the paper, and then place the whole thing on a folded newspaper. Cover it with more newspaper and lay it flat.

Empty the cake pan of water and fill it with sand to form a "plant press" to lay atop the newspaper. When it dries, you'll see that the seaweed has attached itself naturally to the paper.

Seaweed search

Here are different seaweeds that grow in different places. Are any of them at the beach you visit?

GREEN SEAWEEDS:
Sea Moss Seafern
Mermaid's Tresses (also called Green Ball)
Staghorn
Sea Hair

BROWN SEAWEEDS:
Devil's Apron
Gulf Weed

RED SEAWEEDS:
Plumed Chenille
Many Tufted
Agarweed

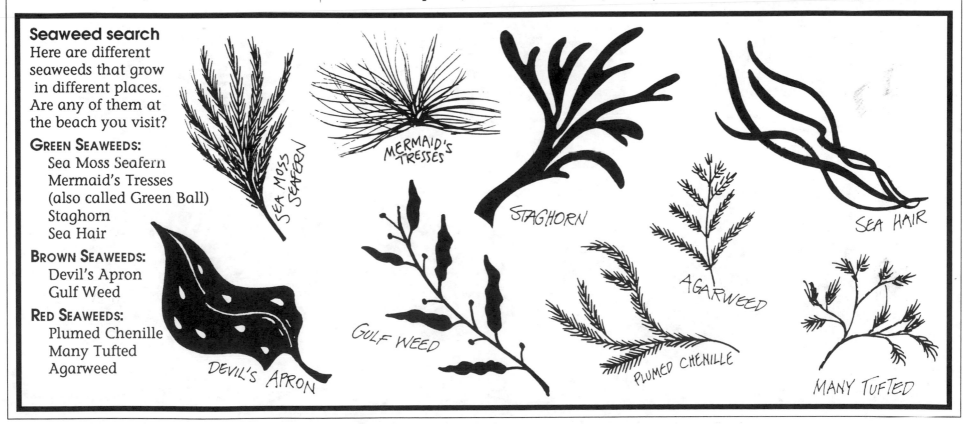

DIVE INTO A TIDE POOL — WITH YOUR EYES, THAT IS

The shallow pools left behind by the sea at low tide are ideal nature observatories. They are home to an awesome array of creatures, both plant and animal. And the fact that the water is so shallow makes them easy to approach.

One caution: be aware of the tides. When the ocean begins to surge back in, it's time to go. Don't linger. The tide pool you are visiting will soon be at the bottom of the ocean.

If you take some of these tidal pool residents out for a visit to your temporary aquarium, be sure to get them back well before high tide. They need time to get shelter before the water comes rushing back in.

TIDAL POND DWELLERS:

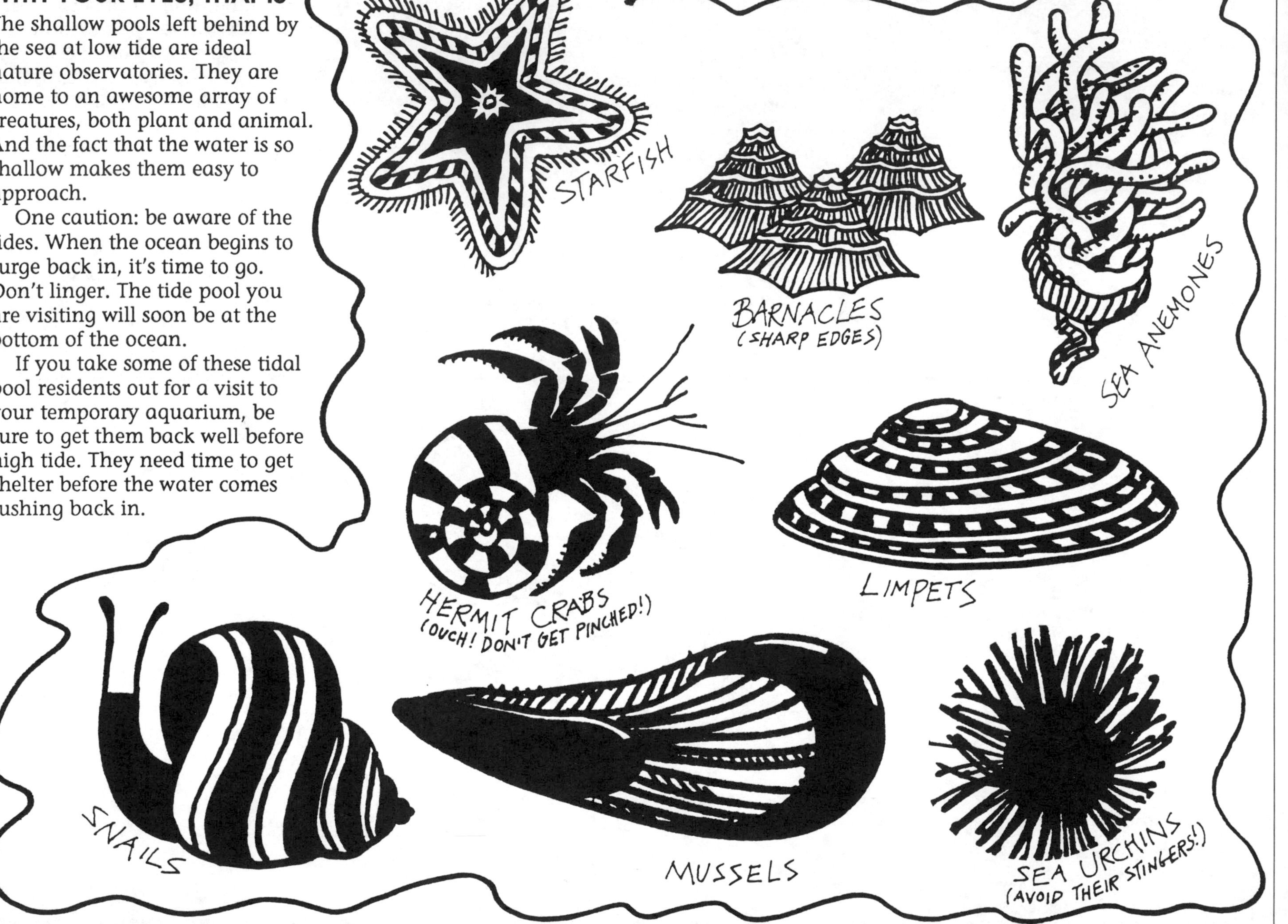

STARFISH

BARNACLES (SHARP EDGES)

SEA ANEMONES

HERMIT CRABS (OUCH! DON'T GET PINCHED!)

LIMPETS

SNAILS

MUSSELS

SEA URCHINS (AVOID THEIR STINGERS!)

SHELL CHIMES

You can make a beautiful wind chime by stringing shells onto a piece of driftwood. Many shells come with tiny holes to hang by. If you need to make a hole in a shell, ask a grown-up to help you heat a small nail. Then, gently hammer it into the shell.

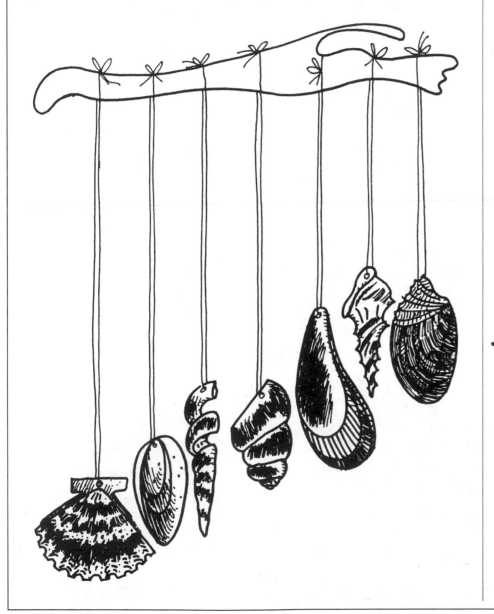

KEEPING IT CLEAN

Sad to say, you may find plain old litter at the beach, too. Some ignorant people dump garbage overboard; some let it drop on the beach. One day they'll learn better, but until they do, people like us need to lend a helping hand clearing garbage from the water and the beach.

Whenever you're at the beach, make it your goal to pick up some litter. It's a great way to say thanks to Mother Nature for letting you visit this wondrous place.

Plastic bags, and the rings from the tops of six-pack containers are the worst offenders. Seabirds, fish, whales, and turtles may mistake them for food, or even get tangled in them and die. Of course, that won't happen with you around!

Join a beach clean up

While you're taking a few minutes to help clean the beach, remember that you're not alone. Beach cleaning has become a global effort involving thousands of people.

A few years ago, over a hundred thousand volunteers cleaned four thousand miles of beaches as part of the Center For Marine Conservation's Great American Trash Off. It's not just for Americans, either. People from other countries take part in beach cleanings, too.

To find out when there'll be an organized cleanup in your area, write or call:
The Center For Marine Conservation
1725 DeSales Street, NW, Suite 600
Washington, DC 20036
202-429-5609

LET'S GO EXPLORING!

Feeling restless? Has the spirit of adventure been bubbling up inside you? Do you picture yourself as the exploring pioneers-type, sailing off to find unknown places?

Maybe it's time you did something about it. Maybe it's time to get out of your house, get off your block, and even leave your neighborhood for the day — to explore the wide world around you — with your parents' permission, of course!

The best part is you don't have to go very far and it doesn't have to cost you anything. There's a world of fascinating things not far from you — places you may have been before, but not as an *explorer*, somebody who sees a place *for the first time*.

How, you ask, can you see a place for the first time, if you've already been there before? The answer is, of course, that you try to see the place *as if* for the first time. You notice things you never noticed before; things strike you in a new way; you get a deeper, fuller understanding of something. You begin to realize that yours is not the only life going on in the world at this moment in time — that there are billions of other people living their lives, all over the world.

We all share the same time frame. It's important that we get to know one another better.

SO HOW ABOUT A VISIT TO . . . .

Your local library

One of the best places in your town to find out what's going on is at the local library. For one thing, there are the books — books which can take you on fantastic journeys into the world of ideas or into the world of make-believe.

But the books are only the beginning of what a library has to offer! For instance, most libraries offer programs for young people. These might include poetry readings or storytelling, movies, lectures and slide shows on all different subjects, performances of music, dance, and drama — all kinds of things!

Then, there's sure to be a bulletin board announcing these programs, in addition to lots of other events going on around town. There may also be pamphlets at the information desk, telling you about all kinds of things being offered.

Before you leave the library, find a map of your area. Start with a map of your town. Can you locate your house or street?

Then ask to see a map of your county. A county map usually has lots of parks and places of interest marked on it. Copy or purchase a good map of your area, and you'll be amazed at what you discover.

Your library can direct you to other places to find out what's going on in your area, too. Places like:

- The town offices
- Parks and Recreation Department
- Board of Education
- Chamber of Commerce

You should call these places during the week before your explore. Some of them are closed on weekends. If there are mailing lists for newsletters listing upcoming events, put your name on them.

A public park

Of course, going to your local park is one of the first things most people think to do on weekends. Parks offer an incredible variety of activities to do in the great outdoors. You can picnic, go bike riding, play at sports, stroll, fly a kite, and birdwatch. In some parks you can hear a concert or people watch. In some you can swim or go boating.

Visit a nature preserve

Every area has at least one nature preserve where people are invited to enjoy the wonders of nature. Check a map or call the Parks Department to find one. Look for a listing of The Nature Conservancy in your phone book. This organization buys land to keep in the natural state, and many of its places are open to the public. For more information, send a postcard to:

> The Nature Conservancy
> 1815 North Lynn Street
> Arlington, VA 22209

When you're in a natural area, remember the old naturalist's credo:

> *Take nothing but pictures,*
> *Leave nothing but footprints,*
> *Spend nothing but time.*

Don't pick flowers or take souvenirs. The natural world is for us all to share and enjoy.

Nature preserves are a perfect place to birdwatch. The best time is late winter and early spring, before the trees have leafed out.

Airport

Chances are there's an airport not too far from where you live. Airports are fascinating places to explore. We live in a small world these days. You can get anywhere in a day or so. What kind of airport is near you? Do flights leave and go to other countries from your airport? Then it's *international*. Where do most of the flights seem to go? How many airlines use the airport, and what are their insignias?

Going back in time

Does the idea of time travel excite you? Then how about a visit back in time — to a restored house or village? Most every area has them. You can find them on a map, or even by looking for Museums or Historical Places in the phone book.

Some restored villages have demonstrations of old-fashioned crafts, like broommaking, blacksmithing, candle dipping, and barrelmaking. You might even get lucky enough to try it yourself!

A visit to some antique stores can be fun, too. You don't have to buy anything, but it's fascinating to see the kinds of things people had, and used, in the old days. The items at antique stores are in varying condition, from tip-top to run-down. If you don't understand what something was for, ask the person at the shop. He'll usually be happy to tell you.

It's a small world after all

Do you know any people from a different country? If you do, you're lucky — you can learn a lot about another culture just by spending time with them. If not, look for International Fairs near you. Schools and colleges sometimes have them. And often, different groups have celebrations to honor the holidays of the countries they came from. For instance, the Irish have St. Patrick's Day, and Brazilians have Carnaval. Sometimes, exhibits about different countries travel to different towns — try to catch one near you. (It's easier if you live near a big city.)

How about people of different religious beliefs? Look in your Yellow Pages under *Churches, Synagogues,* and *Religious Organizations.* There you will find a variety of houses of worship, many of which allow visitors. Are there any mosques? Hindu or Buddhist temples? Jewish synagogues? How about different denominations of Christian churches? Or "New Age" groups?

You may never have been to any kind of religious service but your own. So here's a great explore — pay a visit to a few different houses of worship! Many groups are happy to have visitors, especially if they list the times and places of their ceremonies in the newspaper. Look in the Sunday edition. Or you may want to call ahead and ask if they welcome visitors.

You'll probably find, underneath the differences, that people worship in much the same way. We're more alike than we think, we humans.

Markets

Whether or not you're in the market to buy something, you can have a great look at a wide variety of stuff by going to a market. Everything under the sun may be for sale — both new and used.

If it's food items you're looking for, try a farmer's market. The food will be fresh out of the fields, and it'll taste that way, too. You may come across a vegetable that you've never eaten before. If you're really in the mood to explore, buy a small amount to try at home. You may discover something delicious!

Or how about checking out a flea market? There, people sell all kinds of things, both new and used. Other kinds of stores can be fun to browse in, too — from furniture stores to garden centers, pet stores to hobby shops.

FUN IN THE CAR

If you can walk or ride a bike to where you're going this weekend, fantastic! Or maybe you can reach your destination by taking a train, bus, or boat. That's an adventure in itself! For most of us, though, getting there means hopping in the family car. And sometimes a car trip may seem kind of long.

What can you do to make getting there and back half the fun? How about playing some travel games?

Twenty questions

Twenty questions is a travel game classic. It's fun for everyone to play. Here's how. Someone thinks of something — an object, an animal, a person, whatever. Then, the other people in the car can ask twenty questions to find out what the person is thinking about. The trick is that every question must be answerable by either "yes" or "no."

Here are some typical twenty question questions:
Is what you're thinking of alive?
Is it a plant?
Is it an animal?
Is it as big as a house?
Is it smaller than the car?

Notice that all those questions can be answered by "yes" or "no."

If, after twenty questions have been asked, the answer hasn't yet been revealed, the person thinking of something tells the group, and tries to stump them again with another object. If the group guesses, the person making the correct guess thinks of something herself.

Geography

Everyone takes turns naming a place that could be on a map, like a country, state, city, river, mountain range, ocean, lake, or continent. However, the place you name must start with the last letter of the place named before. For instance, if the person before you said "France" (*ending in E*), you could say "England" (*beginning in E*). If you can't think of anything (that hasn't been said before) when it's your turn, it's either a point against you, or you're out, depending on what rules your group uses.

Ghost

A word game like geography, the idea of Ghost is *not to complete a word*. If you do, you get a G. The second time you do it, you get an H, and so on until you spell GHOST, at which time, you're out of the game. Last one still in the game wins. The first person begins by saying a letter — say, F. The second person says another letter. This letter, and all the letters to follow, must allow for a word to be spelled, but not finish a word. The second person, for instance, can't say P, since there's no word that begins "Fp." So say the second person says E. The third person must add another letter, say, B. If you think there's no word that can be made, you can challenge. If you're right, and there's no such word, the person gets one of the g-h-o-s-t letters. But watch out — if you're wrong, *you* get the letter! In this case, the word *Feb*ruary would make you the loser, if you challenged. Whoever gets a Ghost letter, starts the next word.

Grandma is strange

This classic game gets everyone thinking. Here's how to play. Someone thinks of a secret pecularity of their imaginary Grandma. For instance, what if Grandma only liked words that started with C? Then she would love cats, but hate dogs. She would love carrots, and corn, but hate potatoes and peas.

To begin, the first player mentions one of his Grandmother's strange likes and dislikes. Like, "My grandma is so strange. She loves tomatoes, but hates cake. And she's crazy for onions, but hates ice cream!" The other players must guess the secret underlying grandma's likes and dislikes. In the example above, grandma only liked words that had "O" in them. If one of the other players guesses the combination, she can test out her idea. In the example above, she might ask, "Does your grandma love opera, and hate rap?" If the player realizes she's guessed grandma's strange secret, she, too, joins the first player, giving the other players clues.

Grandma can love words with double letters, or things that are only one color, or animals with four legs — you name it.

Grandmother's trunk

Another Grandma game! This game just gets better and better the more things are found in grandmother's trunk. Here's how it works:

The first player says, "My grandmother has a trunk. And in her trunk are apples." Now it's the next player's turn. "My grandmother has a trunk. And in her trunk are apples and books." The third player might say, "My grandmother has a trunk, and in her trunk are apples, books, and carrots."

Do you see what's happening here? Everyone is repeating the list in order, and adding a word that begins with the next letter in the alphabet.

You've got to remember everything in grandmother's trunk — in order — before you can add a new word!

Dear Pen Pal, Today is Saturday...

Your Friend

Here's a quiz with just four questions for you to answer. Answer each question Yes or No.

1. ❏ Do you like to make new friends?

2. ❏ Are you interested in how other people, in faraway places, live?

3. ❏ Do you enjoy receiving mail?

4. ❏ Can you keep a promise?

If you said yes to all four questions, then you are a good candidate for having, and being, a pen pal.

HOW TO FIND A PEN PAL

There are many different organizations that can help you find a pen pal. Some offer their services for free; others charge a small fee. With some, you can ask for a pen pal in a specific country or state; with others, you are simply assigned a pen pal from somewhere in the world. There are special pen pal organizations for school kids, pet lovers, and even science fiction buffs.

World Pen Pals
PO Box 337
Saugerties, NY 12477
914-246-7828

Kids ten and over send name, address, age, sex, and SASE (self-addressed, stamped envelope). Include the $3.00 fee, and which sex and home continent you prefer for your pen pal.

Russian pen pals

You can play a special part in promoting world peace by having a pen pal from Russia. There are many Russian children and grown-ups interested in writing to English-speaking pen friends, so they can practice their English and make new friends at the same time.

An American organization, *Peace Links*, will help you find a Russian pen pal at absolutely no charge. They also have lists of groups of kids in schools that want to get in touch with English-speaking pen pals. You can get your whole class involved.

There's no charge for a Peace Links Pen Pal. For more information write to:

Peace Links Pen Pals for Peace
729 Eighth St. SE, Suite 300
Washington, DC 20003

E-pals

Join the new age of correspondence by finding a pen pal through the Internet. The *Student Letter Exchange* (http://www.pen-pal.com) offers four free pen pals per year. Pen pals will be your age and sex.

You won't even need stationery when you get a pen pal at the *Cyber Kids Pen Pal Page* (http://www. cyberzone.on.ca/kids/pals/ guestbook.html) — just your keyboard. Simply read the pen pal descriptions, choose one you like, click on his or her e-mail address, and type away. You can also post information about yourself on the page.

Here are some ideas about what to put in that very first letter.

➦ Tell your pen pal where you live and who lives with you.

➦ Tell him about school, and what your favorite subjects are and why.

➦ If you have any hobbies or special interests, let your pen pal know about them. The things you like to do will say a lot about the kind of person you are, giving your pen pal something to respond to.

➦ Ask your pen pal about herself, what she likes to do, what she likes to study, and so on. The more you show an interest in your pen pal's life, the more she will feel free to respond.

➦ It never hurts to remind your pen pal that you are looking forward to getting a letter back, either. And remember to promise to write back! Then, be sure to keep your promise.

➦ Don't forget to include your complete address. Imagine some-one trying to write back to Chris in New York City!

Writing the first letter may be fun, but as time goes by, your correspondence with your pen pal will grow even more rewarding. It's great to know that there are people in faraway places who know and care about you! And even more important, in time you'll come to care about them.

MAKE YOUR OWN STATIONERY

You can create special stationery with a potato stamper. Cut a potato in half. Carve out a shape, such as a star, or triangle. Dip the shape you created in poster or tempura paint.

Try creating a repeating border. Experiment on scrap paper until you find a design you like the best. Then stamp the potato onto a piece of fresh writing paper and a clean envelope, and let it dry in a flat position. Voila! Handmade stationery that's completely unique, and created by you!

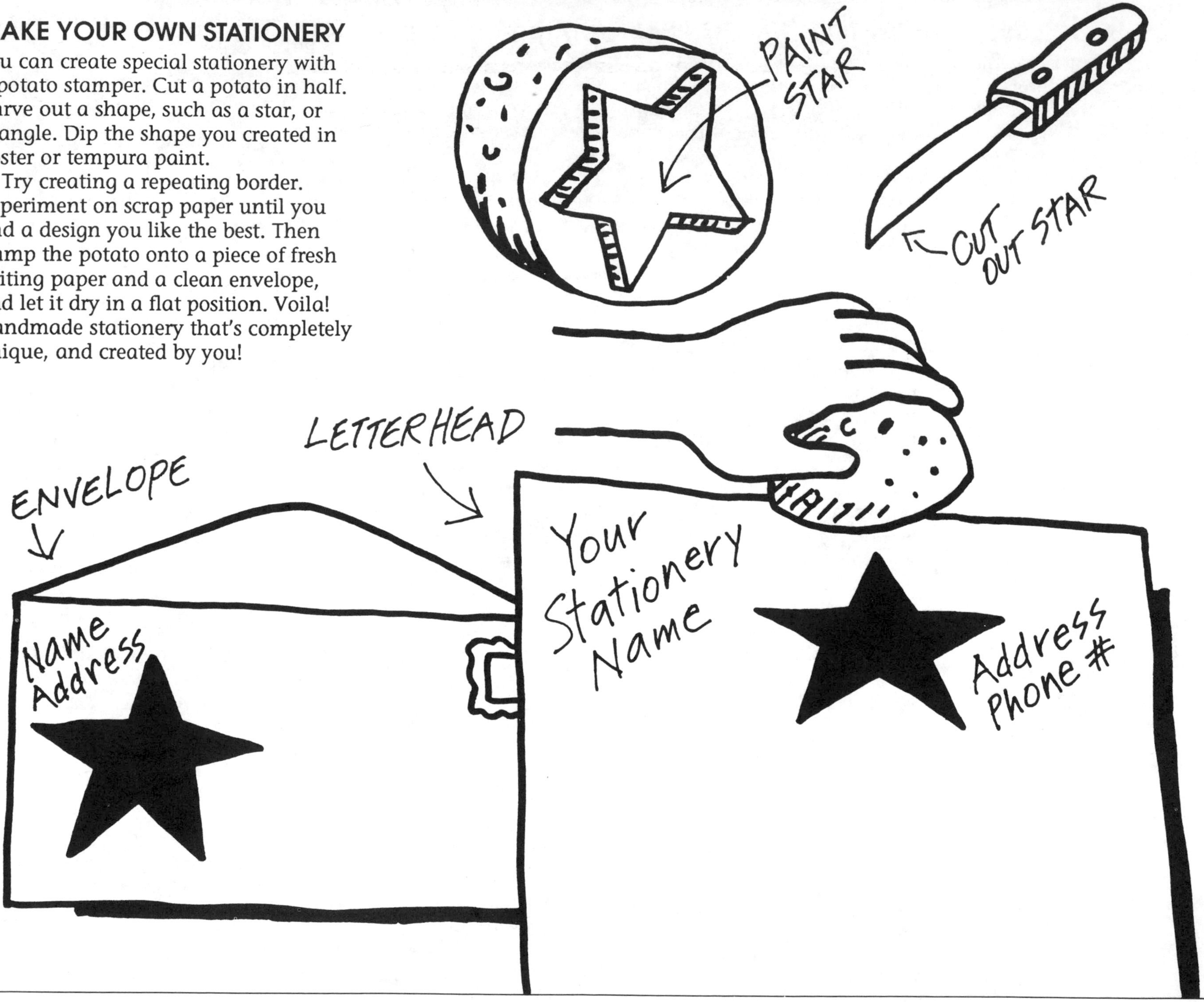

PAINT STAR

CUT OUT STAR

LETTERHEAD

ENVELOPE

Name
Address

Your
Stationery
Name

Address
Phone #

WRITE AWAY FOR FREE STUFF

★★★★

The United States Government will send you information for free! They give away booklets on all sorts of subjects, and all you have to do to get one is to request it! The pamphlet you will receive will have been paid for by United States taxpayers — in other words, by United States grown-ups!

You can get a complete list at your local library. Ask for the government's *Consumer Information Catalogue*, and the librarian will give you one. Write for any of the titles listed and send to:

Consumer Information Center
Pueblo, CO 81009

Include just one dollar for up to twenty-five booklets (for all, not each. This helps Uncle Sam pay for postage.) Make sure your full name and address, with zip code, are included when you make your requests.

Here are few examples of booklets you can receive:
Action Guide to Healthy Eating
Deputy Fire Marshal Kit
Fitness and Exercise
Growing Up Drug Free
Preventing Childhood Poisoning
The Duck Stamp Story
Why Save Endangered Species?

TRAVEL THE WIDE WORLD

Got the travel bug? Even if you can't call for tickets today, many tourism offices around the globe will be happy to provide information about their country, and what makes it so special. Send them a postcard asking for tourist information. When they send the packet to you, you can start your sightseeing right at home!

Use a postcard to make your request. Be sure to include your full name and address, including zip code.

Write to:

Belgian National Tourist Office
780 3rd Ave., Ste. 1501
NY, NY 10151

Danish Tourist Board
Box 4649, Grand Central Station
NY, NY 10163

Egyptian Tourist Authority
630 Fifth Ave., Ste. 1706
NY, NY 10111
(comes with a hieroglyphic chart!)

Finnish Tourist Board
Box 4649, Grand Central Station
NY, NY 10163

French Government Tourist Office
444 Madison Ave., 16th Fl.
NY, NY 10022

German National Tourist Office
122 E. 42nd St., 52nd Fl.
NY, NY 10168

Greek National Tourist Organization
645 Fifth Ave.
NY, NY 10022

Irish Tourist Board
590 Fifth Ave.
NY, NY 10036

Italian Government Travel Office
666 Fifth Ave.
NY, NY 10111

Portuguese National Tourist Office
590 Fifth Ave., 4th Fl.
NY, NY 10036

Tourist Office of Spain
666 Fifth Ave., 35th Fl.
NY, NY 10022

Swedish Tourist Board
Box 4649, Grand Central Station
NY, NY 10163

RAINY DAY BRIGHTENERS

Classy Gifts to Make

Weekends are the perfect time for making gifts for the special people in your life. And since you're giving, why not give the best? Here are some suggestions for classy gifts to make for classy people — people like your family, friends, and even yourself!

SCENTED BATH SALTS

If you know someone who likes to luxuriate in the bath, relaxing in a tub of perfumed, silky water, then this is the perfect gift! It doesn't cost much to make, but it sure *seems* expensive!

What you'll need:

Epsom salts*

Glycerin*

Food coloring

Cologne, perfume, rosewater, or other fragrance

A jar

Ribbon, or lace

Paint, or fabric to cover the lid of the jar

A glass or metal bowl

Liquid soap (optional)

*buy at any pharmacy

This formula uses three cups of Epsom salts to one tablespoon of glycerin. It makes enough bath salts to fill one to three medium-sized jars.

Begin by getting the gift jar ready. (Jam and jelly jars are often pretty to look at.) Decorate the lid by painting it, or by glueing on a round piece of pretty fabric that will later be tied with ribbon or lace.

In a cup, mix the glycerin and food coloring. Use only one or two drops of each color. (If the salts are dark, they may look nice in the jar. But remember, the person bathing in them may not wish to turn a bright color!) One or two drops of yellow, and an equal amount of red, make a lovely peach color. A drop or two of blue, and an equal amount of green,

make a pretty seafoam aqua. If you know the person's favorite color, or what color his or her bathroom is, try matching it.

To the glycerin and coloring, add a few drops of perfume or any other liquid fragrance.

Pour the fragrant, colored glycerin into a large bowl and add the Epsom salts. Gently stir the two substances with your fingers until the salts are all the same color. Use a gentle motion with your fingertips, as if you are giving a shampoo.

For foaming bath salts, combine two tablespoons of liquid soap with only one teaspoon of glycerin. You may need to add more Epsom salts, if the bath salts look heavy.

When the salts are mixed, fill a jar, and tie it with ribbon or lace. What a classy gift!

A PRESSED FLOWER (OR SEAWEED) TRAY

You'll need:

An old picture frame

A set of handles*

Pressed flowers or seaweed

*purchase at a hardware store

Remove any hardware on the back of the frame so that the back is smooth. Place pressed flowers, or seaweed into the frame. Then attach handles to the shorter sides of the frame with small screws.

To make pressed flowers, pick some and put them between two sheets of waxed paper. Place the waxed paper between the pages of a heavy book. After a few weeks, the flowers will be dried, pressed, and ready.

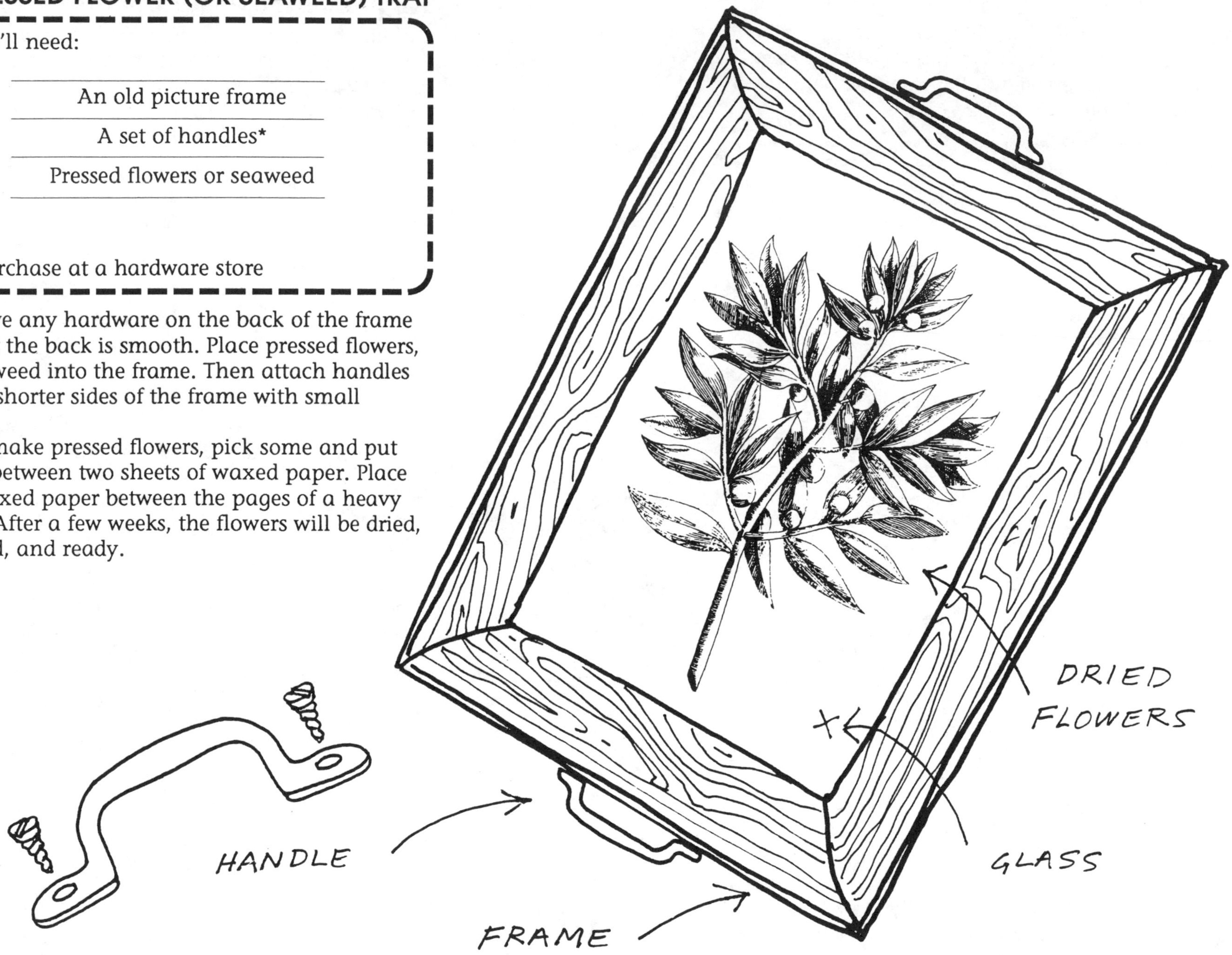

HANDLE

FRAME

DRIED FLOWERS

GLASS

BUGLE BEADS (ENLARGED)

BARRETTE BACK

FINISHED BARRETTE

BUGLE BEAD BARRETTES AND MATCHING PIN

In a fabric or hobby shop, buy a package or two of bugle beads, a pin back, and a pair of barrette backs. These are all inexpensive. Open the bugle beads and spread them out on a piece of scrap paper. The beads should be close together, touching but not overlapping.

Next, spread white glue onto the back of the pin and the two barrettes. Make sure that every bit of the surface is covered with glue.

Dip the barrette and pin backs onto the bugle beads. Don't worry if there seems to be too much glue — the white color will disappear as the glue dries.

Place the beaded barrettes and pin back on an open shelf to dry, and leave them there overnight. The hardest part of this project is *not touching* what you've made until the glue is thoroughly dry! The next morning, look for a beautiful set of barrettes and a matching pin. This gift will last!

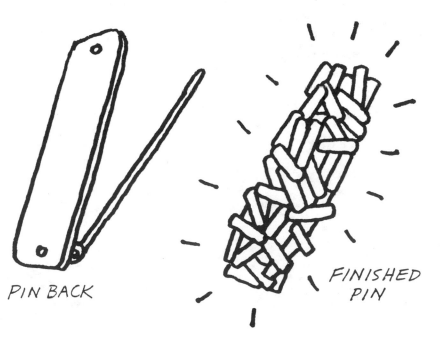

PIN BACK

FINISHED PIN

FOR THAT SPECIAL CAT — A CATNIP BALL

Fill the toe of an old nylon stocking with catnip and tie it closed. Add a jingle bell to the thread you tie it with, for extra effect. Attach the ball and bell to a piece of elastic, which can be purchased in any fabric or sewing shop. The elastic should be at least a yard long. (If you can't get to a store, make an elastic string by tying rubber bands together.)

To play, place the ball on the ground a few feet from the cat, but act like you're not even aware of it. When the cat spies the ball and comes over to sniff it, gently yank it away a few inches. Cats like a good challenge. Continue teasing the cat with the catnip ball, but don't let her get too frustrated. After all, everybody likes to win, even Puss!

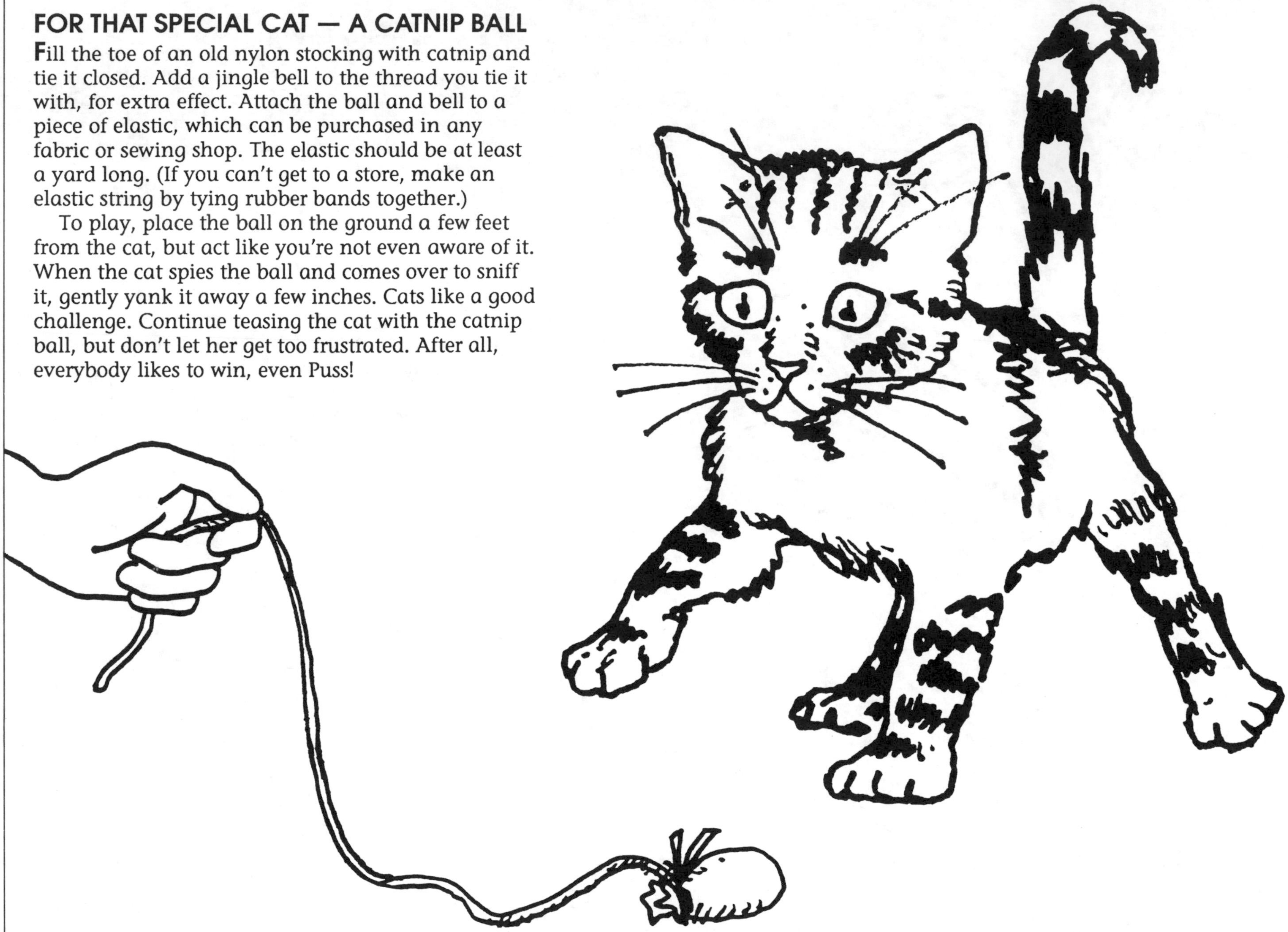

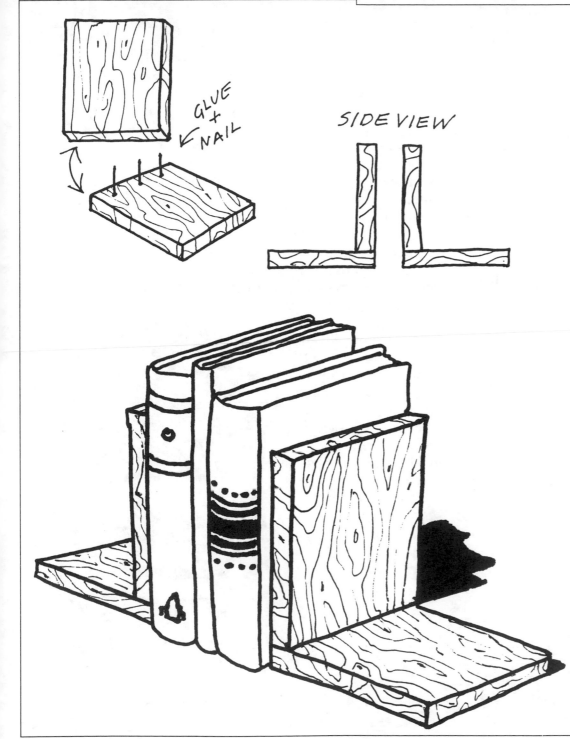

GLUE + NAIL

SIDE VIEW

CLASSY WOOD-GRAIN BOOKENDS

For this simple woodworking project you'll need:

A hammer

A ruler

A pencil

Four pieces of soft wood (like pine or fir), approximately 4" x 5" (10 cm x 12.5 cm)

Two pieces of felt or non-skid tape

Sandpaper: coarse, medium, and fine

Six finishing nails, at least 1 1/2" (3.5 cm) long

The pieces of wood you use for these bookends can be whatever size you have. The measurements here are just guidelines.

Start by sanding the wood until it is smooth to the touch. Pay special attention to the ends of the wood. First, sand them with coarse sandpaper, then medium, then fine.

When the wood is smooth, draw a line across the wood, 1/2" (1 cm) from one of the short sides, and mark three evenly spaced places along it. Hammer three nails in those marks so that they just pop out of the other side.

Put glue along the edge of the other piece of wood. Then hold the glued piece upright (you may need help to do this), and place the other edge, with the nails sticking out, in the center of it. Tap the nails all the way in, connecting the two pieces of wood.

You can jazz the bookends up by painting and decorating them, but the natural grain of the wood may be beautiful just as it is. Judge for yourself.

To bring out the beauty of the wood grain, and finish the wood so it will resist dirt, rub the bookends with oil or furniture paste wax.

MAKE A JAPANESE SERVING TABLE

To make this classy little table, which is used for serving food, you'll need three pieces of scrap wood. The exact measurement isn't important, as long as the width is about two-thirds of the length. For example, your table might be a foot (30 cm) long, and eight inches (20 cm) wide.

On the biggest piece of wood, draw two lines (which the legs will be under) and mark three evenly spaced Xs on them. Make your marks lightly with a pencil. Later, you'll erase them.

Nail finishing nails into the marks until they poke through the other side.

Put glue along the legs, and hold each one as you hammer the nails in. Do this on both sides of the table.

Wipe away any extra glue and then sand the table. You can oil it with vegetable oil to give it a polished look. Don't use furniture wax, though, since food may be put on it.

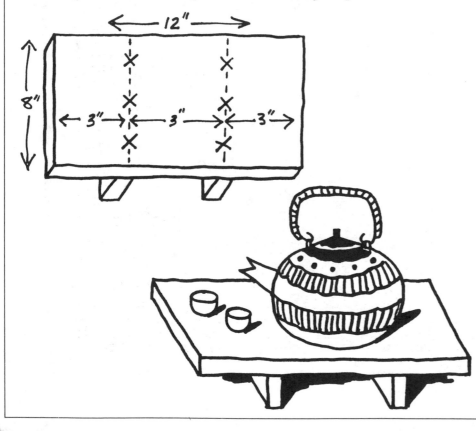

RAINBOW GIFTWRAP — FOR FREE!

Part of the thrill of getting a great gift is unwrapping it! You can make awesome rainbow giftwrap from brown paper bags and poster paint. You'll need red, yellow, blue, and green.

Start by painting the bottom of the bags any color you like. (Making several bags at once is a good idea. After all, you already have the supplies out.)

When the bottom is dry, flatten the bag and start painting horizontal stripes on it. The stripes can be wide or narrow. Do one side of the bag at a time, allowing each side to dry. If you put it in the sun, it will only take a few minutes, but if you're in a super-hurry, get a grown-up to blow it with a hair dryer. Don't be afraid to use plenty of paint. Also, if the colors run together, don't worry — it only makes the paper better.

To get the rainbow effect, repeat this order of colors: red, orange, yellow, green, blue, purple. Make orange by mixing red and yellow. Make purple by mixing blue and red.

Let the bag dry, then wrap the gift inside and tie the top with ribbon or yarn. You've just created gorgeous rainbow giftwrap. And all it cost was your time!

HOMEY HEIRLOOM HOUSE

This gift is super-special for anyone who likes the place they live! It's a picture of their house, cut from fabric, like the old-fashioned heirlooms of last century. The measurements here are just given as guidelines. The materials you have on hand will determine the size.

You'll need a piece of plywood or very firm cardboard, as big as the picture you want to create. You'll also need fabric and glue. Felt is the very best kind of fabric to use, and calico prints are nice, too, but any material scraps will do.

Start by drawing a simple picture of the person's house. You can work from a photo, if you have one, or from memory, if you are daring.

Using the picture as a guideline, cut shapes from your material scraps to reconstruct the picture on the plywood. For instance, you may have green material to represent a lawn, white material to represent a white house, red material to represent bricks. Windows and doors can be represented by black, if you like.

Before you begin glueing the scraps to the plywood, construct the whole house, putting the setting first (like the lawn, or a hill). Light blue material makes a nice daytime sky, and black makes for a good nighttime background. Add cotton ball clouds, or sticker stars, if you like. Glue the background, and don't be afraid of using too much glue. It will dry clear. Add a tree to the "front yard" if you like.

When you have glued the entire "house" in its setting onto the plywood, let it dry overnight. The next day, you can glue or nail straight sticks to the edge of the plywood to make a homemade frame.

GLITTER &

You can add real sparkle to your life with glitter and sequins! And nothing makes a rainy day seem brighter.

Turn your next rainy weekend into a glitter and sequin show! Little kids, big kids — even senior citizen kids — all like shaking the shiny stuff and dressing up with a little flash.

Glitter drawings

Use an old brush to "paint" pictures with glue. Then sprinkle glitter all over it. Work inside a tray to avoid a sparkly mess!

To use more than one color of glitter, paint parts of the picture separately, and glitterize them one at a time. Let the glue dry before continuing.

Try a portrait or self-portait. Or how about a glittering group portrait of your family or friends?

Glitter shakers

Little kids love these, and they make good gifts for young ones, too. Use a cleaned-out baby food jar or other small jar.

Add a tablespoon of glitter and fill the jar with water, not all the way to the top, but most of the way. Put glue on the inside threads of the jar lid, and close the jar tightly. You can add a marble, or anything small and waterproof, but you don't have to. The glitter itself will be fun to look at.

When the lid is dry, take the shaker to a sunny place, turn it upside down, and shake!

A glittery picture frame

Take a small frame, 3" x 5" (7.5 cm x 12.5 cm) or so. One by one, smear the sides with glue, and shake on glitter. The next day, or after it's thoroughly dry, paint it again with clear nail polish, shellac, or varnish. (Younger kids, please get permission.) Talk about adding sparkle to your life!

SEQUINS

SEQUINS

Do you wish your clothes had a little more sparkle? Put sequins on them and they will! You can sequin any material, even canvas. So think about your sneakers — how would they look with a little sparkle and flash?

You can purchase sequins at any fabric store and most variety shops. Use them to give your clothes a fabulous new look.

A sequined T-shirt

Attaching sequins to a T-shirt couldn't be easier. You don't need any fancy tools to do it, either! A plain old teaspoon works fine.

Push the back of the sequin, the part with the prongs, through the underside of the material, so that the prongs jut out in the front. Then, drop the sequin into the prongs and push the prongs down on it, one by one, around the sequin.

Now you get to design! Will you try a pattern, like a sun? Or just have the sequins appear scattered, like a starry night?

For something extra wild, how about *painting* the fabric first, and then using sequins to fill the drawing in?

Here you can really let your creativity fly! Will you paint bright city lights? Sparkles on a lake? A traffic jam? A Native American symbol?

You can find painted, sequined clothes items in the choicest city boutiques. There they sell for hundreds of dollars! And just think, you can make yours for just the cost of the sequins!

THE FAMILY PHOTOS

There's nothing like sitting around a table looking through the family photos, and the weekend is the perfect time to do it. Just open up the album or the box where your family keeps them, and something magical will happen! The past will reappear before your eyes in the form of pictures taken over the years — Grandma when she was young, you as a baby, Mom as a teen, Dad at his wedding. It's all there!

Protecting photos

In order to last, photos should be kept in a dry, dark place that's not exposed to too much heat. Never store photos by a heater or a sunny window. Avoid stacking them, too — especially if they're lying down.

A few no-nos

Looking at the family photos will be more fun if you pay attention to a few important rules.

1. No drinks at the table! That delicious glass of lemonade is a lethal weapon when there are photos around.

2. No grabbing.

3. Handle the photos by their edges to avoid getting fingerprints on them.

ORGANIZING AN ALBUM

Why not take a weekend to put your family's photos in good order? There are lots of ways to do it, and when it's done, you'll have the resulting album to treasure for years.

You can buy inexpensive albums at most variety stores. The cheapest have sticky pages, over which a piece of clear plastic is laid. These look great when you first put the album together, but after a few years, the sticky pages dry up and the photos slide out. Still, putting them in this kind of album is better than stuffing them in a box.

What goes where?

You can take a few different approaches when organizing your album. Here are some ideas:

Do a time sequence. Start with the earliest photos and keep adding them as they were taken. You don't have to include every photo. You can select the best, and store the rest. Or, make more than one album to keep or give to other family members.

Highlight the individual. How about a page or more focusing on each family member, using photos of them in which they are alone? You could have a picture of the person as a baby, a toddler, and so on. It's fascinating to see a person's development reflected right there on the page!

Group around events. Try putting all the graduation pictures together, or all the vacation shots, or holiday and party shots, together.

Don't forget the house. It's interesting to see how your house has looked through the years, if you've always lived there. Or, group together pictures of the various places you've lived, if your family has moved.

MAKE A PHOTO ALBUM FROM SCRATCH

It's not difficult to construct a photo album that will last for many years. A homemade album will protect your photos while displaying them beautifully. Making an album is a great classy gift, too. (See *The Book of Me*, page 36, for more book-making suggestions.)

PUTTING IT ALL TOGETHER

1. Carefully mark and punch out holes on the edges of the paper, and reinforce them. Since your pages will be oversized, use more than three holes, but not so many that the book will be bound too tightly. Six to eight is a good number.

2. Select the photos you want to use. Experiment to find the best groupings by placing the photos on the pages without attaching them. When you have the photos the way you want them, mark the corners lightly with a pencil. Then moisten and paste on the corner tabs, and carefully slide each picture in. Only use one side of the paper, so that your photos will not touch other photos when the album is closed.

3. Attach the pages by sewing through the punched holes loosely with yarn or thin ribbon. Allow enough so that the pages turn easily without sliding apart. Tie with a bow or knot.

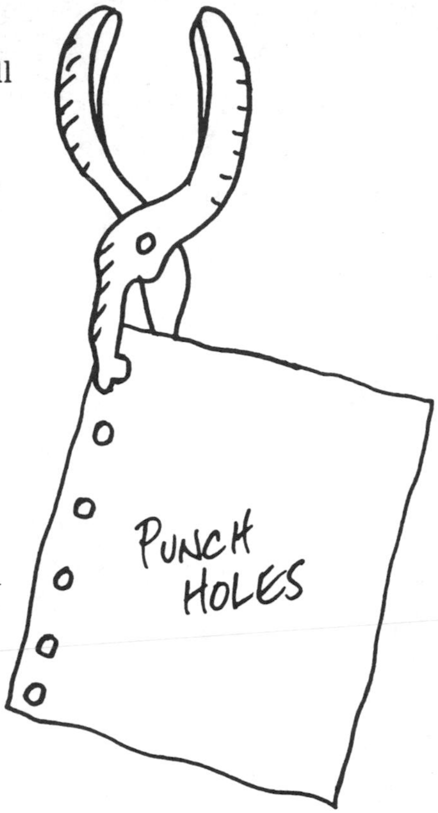

PUNCH HOLES

MAKE LAYOUT

RIBBON OR YARN →

FAMILY PHOTO ALBUM

YOU'LL NEED:

Several large sheets of good quality, stiff paper. It's best to go for quality in this case, since your album will last for many years. Buy high-quality paper at an art supply store. Use white or natural color paper so that the photos won't be hurt by dyes.

Photo tabs. These are the triangular, pre-pasted corners. Get a good supply because each photo requires four tabs.

A large, flat work space with good light

A hole puncher, hole reinforcers

Thin ribbon or thick yarn to tie the album together

Clean hands

Weekends are a great time to explore the world of food and cooking. Learning to put a meal together is a satisfying — and delicious — activity. Rainy days seem to be a great time for the family to pitch in together. So here are some simple ideas for things to cook up:

SPAGHETTI LALLAPALOOZA

Here's a truly tasty spaghetti dinner that's nutritious, delicious, and easy for a family to fix. It's Spaghetti Lallapalooza, with salad and garlic bread or Italian toast. Serve with natural grape soda. This meal is simple enough for older kids to make on their own. If you are old enough to use the stove, see if you can get Mom and Dad out of the kitchen one night of the weekend!

You'll need:

One onion, or four stalks of scallions

Three cloves of garlic

One pound (.5 kg) of mushrooms

A tablespoon (15 ml) of oil

One can of red or white kidney beans, drained

One quart (1 L) of sugarless spaghetti sauce

One pound (.5 kg) of spaghetti

Put a large pot of water on the stove to boil while you prepare the other ingredients.

Slice or chop the onion, mushrooms, and garlic. (If you cut the onion under running water, your eyes won't burn.) Heat the oil in a skillet, and add the chopped vegetables. Cook on a medium flame for five minutes. Add the pre-cooked sauce, and the can of drained beans.

Simmer the sauce until the spaghetti is cooked. Drain and serve. Serves 4-8.

Salad

Salad
Lettuce
Tomatoes
Cucumber
Parsley

Tear up two big leaves of lettuce for each person eating. Cut up one or two tomatoes to put on top of the lettuce. Slice cucumbers to fringe the bowl. Tear off about a half a cup (125 ml) of parsley in small pieces, and put it around the bowl. For dressing, squeeze the juice of a lemon over the salad.

Italian toast

Slice a loaf of Italian bread the long way, and pull out some of the soft insides. (This makes good food for the birds. Just toss it onto the lawn in little pieces). Smear the bread with a little margarine. Toast under the broiler for just a couple of minutes.

For the brave — garlic bread

Cut three or four cloves of garlic into as thin slices or tiny pieces as you can. Melt a half a stick of margarine, and add the chopped garlic. Smear this mixture on a loaf of Italian bread, broil, and eat. If you like garlic, but not the garlicky aftertaste, munch on a sprig of parsley at the end of the dinner.

For dessert — fruit salad

You'd better make plenty of this fruit salad. It goes quickly!

YOU'LL NEED:

Two bananas
Two oranges
Sugarless pineapple (any kind)
An apple

Plus any other fruit you like and can easily get. For instance — grapes, melon, pears, strawberries, pieces of cherries, blueberries — you choose. If you can get some unsweetened coconut to sprinkle on top, so much the better. (Most health food stores have it.)

Peel the fruit that needs peeling. (The peels make great compost.)

Wash the fruit that needs washing.

Cut or slice all the fruit. If you have permission to work with a knife, slice and cut away from your body.

Serve in a large bowl. Scrumptious!

YOU'LL NEED:

- Whole wheat bread (2-3 slices for each person)
- Two eggs (Or better yet, a carton of egg substitute)
- Cinnamon
- 1 tablespoon (15 ml) of oil
- A couple of drops of vanilla extract
- Real maple syrup, or all-fruit syrup

BRILLIANT BRUNCHES

Breakfast plus lunch equals brunch. And about the only time brunch is eaten is on the weekend! Why not start a family tradition of something special for brunch every weekend? You deserve it!

Here's a recipe for French Toast that everyone loves!

Crack the eggs into a pie plate or shallow bowl. Sprinkle on a healthy dose of cinnamon. Add a drop or two of vanilla if you have it. Stir it all with a fork. Begin heating the oil in a skillet.

Dip the bread in the mixture, turning it so both sides are dipped. Put it into the heated oil. After a minute, turn it over. Cook until lightly browned.

Serve with syrup, and enjoy!

MAKE PRETZELS

YOU'LL NEED:

Clean hands!

2 cups (500 ml) whole wheat flour

1 tablespoon (15 ml) vegetable oil

1 tablespoon (15 ml) (1 package) active dry yeast

3/4 cup (175 ml) lukewarm fruit juice (apple, cherry, orange)

1 egg

Pretzel salt (optional)

Here's a rainy day brightener everyone will like! These soft, whole wheat pretzels are easy to make — and even easier to eat!

Put the flour, oil, yeast, and juice in a large bowl. Mix it all together and then knead it by pushing, pulling and punching it. If the pretzel dough is sticky, add more flour.

Tear off a piece of dough and use the palms of your hands to roll it into a long snake. Some kids stop right there, making Pretzel Snakes. You can shape your snake into an infinity sign, too (It looks like a figure 8 on its side). Use your imagination to create pretzel creatures, or just bake the dough as sticks — it's up to you!

When you have the shapes you like, put them on a lightly oiled cookie sheet. Let the dough rise for 30 minutes in a warm place.

Pre-heat the oven to 450°F (230°C). Then, beat the egg and brush it over the pretzels. Add salt if you want (these pretzels are yummy even without it, though.)

Bake the pretzels for 15 minutes, or until they are golden brown. Let them cool down, then eat them up!

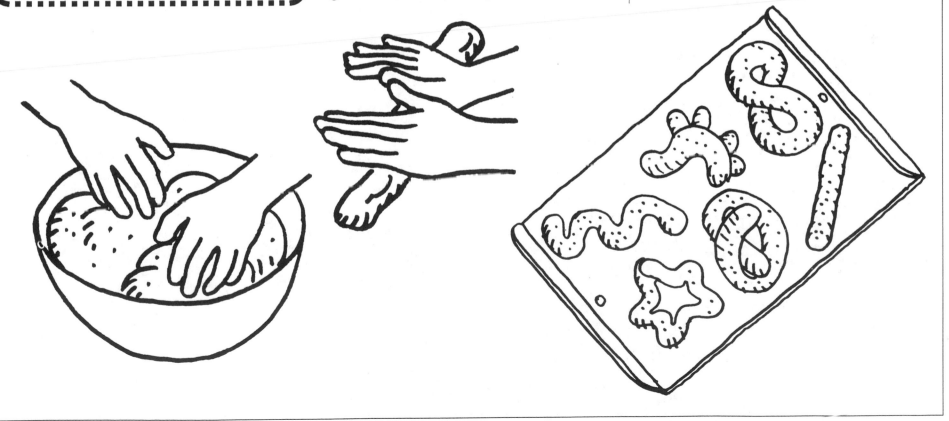

MORE GOOD BOOKS FROM WILLIAMSON PUBLISHING

Kids Can!®

The following Kids Can!® books for ages 4 to 10 are each 160-178 pages, fully illustrated, trade paper, 11 x 8 ¹/₂, $12.95 US.

HAND-PRINT ANIMAL ART
 by Carolyn Carreiro ($14.95)

CUT-PAPER PLAY!
Dazzling Creations from Construction Paper
 by Sandi Henry

Early Childhood News Directors' Choice Award
VROOM! VROOM!
Making 'dozers, 'copters, trucks & more
 by Judy Press

COOL CRAFTS & AWESOME ART!
A Kids' Treasure Trove of Fabulous Fun
 by Roberta Gould

Oppenheim Toy Portfolio Best Book Award
American Bookseller Pick of the Lists
Benjamin Franklin Best Nonfiction Award
SUPER SCIENCE CONCOCTIONS
50 Mysterious Mixtures for Fabulous Fun
 by Jill Frankel Hauser

Dr. Toy Best Vacation Product
Parents' Choice Gold Award
Parents Magazine Parents' Pick
THE KIDS' NATURE BOOK *(Newly Revised)*
365 Indoor/Outdoor Activities and Experiences
 by Susan Milord

Benjamin Franklin Best Multicultural Book Award
Parents' Choice Approved
Skipping Stones Multicultural Honor Award
THE KIDS' MULTICULTURAL COOKBOOK
Food & Fun Around the World
 by Deanna F. Cook

KIDS' COMPUTER CREATIONS
Using Your Computer for Art & Craft Fun
 by Carol Sabbeth

Parents' Choice Approved
Dr. Toy Best Vacation Product Award
KIDS GARDEN!
The Anytime, Anyplace Guide to Sowing & Growing Fun
 by Avery Hart and Paul Mantell

Winner of the Oppenheim Toy Portfolio Best Book Award
American Bookseller Pick of the Lists
THE KIDS' SCIENCE BOOK
Creative Experiences for Hands-On Fun
 by Robert Hirschfeld and Nancy White

Parents' Choice Gold Award
American Bookseller Pick of the Lists
Winner of the Oppenheim Toy Portfolio Best Book Award
THE KIDS' MULTICULTURAL ART BOOK
Art & Craft Experiences from Around the World
 by Alexandra M. Terzian

Parents' Choice Gold Award
Benjamin Franklin Best Juvenile Nonfiction Award
KIDS MAKE MUSIC!
Clapping and Tapping from Bach to Rock
  by Avery Hart and Paul Mantell

American Bookseller Pick of the Lists
KIDS' CRAZY CONCOCTIONS
50 Mysterious Mixtures for Art & Craft Fun
  by Jill Frankel Hauser

Winner of the Oppenheim Toy Portfolio Best Book Award
Skipping Stones Nature & Ecology Honor Award
EcoArt!
Earth-Friendly Art & Craft Experiences for 3- to 9-Year-Olds
  by Laurie Carlson

KIDS COOK!
Fabulous Food for the Whole Family
  by Sarah Williamson and Zachary Williamson

THE KIDS' WILDLIFE BOOK
Exploring Animal Worlds through Indoor/Outdoor
Crafts & Experiences
  by Warner Shedd

HANDS AROUND THE WORLD
365 Creative Ways to Build Cultural Awareness & Global Respect
  by Susan Milord

KIDS CREATE!
Art & Craft Experiences for 3- to 9-Year-Olds
  by Laurie Carlson

Parents Magazine Parents' Pick
KIDS LEARN AMERICA!
Bringing Geography to Life with People, Places, & History
  by Patricia Gordon and Reed C. Snow

American Bookseller Pick of the Lists
ADVENTURES IN ART *(Newly Revised)*
Art & Craft Experiences for 8- to 13-Year-Olds
  by Susan Milord

Little Hands®

**The following *Little Hands*® books for ages 2 to 6
are each 144 pages, fully illustrated, trade paper,
10 x 8, $12.95 US.**

MATH PLAY!
80 Ways to Count & Learn
  by Diane McGowan and Mark Schrooten

American Bookseller Pick of the Lists
RAINY DAY PLAY!
Explore, Create, Discover, Pretend
  by Nancy Fusco Castaldo

STOP, LOOK & LISTEN
Using Your Senses from Head to Toe
  by Sarah A. Williamson

Children's BOMC Main Selection
THE LITTLE HANDS ART BOOK
Exploring Arts & Crafts with 2- to 6-Year-Olds
  by Judy Press

Parents' Choice Approved
Early Childhood News Directors' Choice Award
SHAPES, SIZES, & MORE SURPRISES!
A Little Hands Early Learning Book
  by Mary Tomczyk

Parents' Choice Approved
The Little Hands BIG FUN CRAFT Book
Creative Fun for 2- to 6-Year-Olds
  by Judy Press

Parents' Choice Approved
THE LITTLE HANDS NATURE BOOK
Earth, Sky, Critters & More
  by Nancy Fusco Castaldo

OTHER BOOKS FROM WILLIAMSON PUBLISHING